EX·LIBRIS

The Byzantine Tradition in
Church Embroidery

The Salonica epitaphios. Detail, *The Communion of the Apostles.* 14th century. (Byzantine Museum, Athens.) (see also Pls. 95, 96.)

THE
BYZANTINE TRADITION
IN
CHURCH EMBROIDERY

PAULINE JOHNSTONE

ARGONAUT, INC., PUBLISHERS
CHICAGO   MCMLXVII

FIRST AMERICAN EDITION PUBLISHED BY ARGONAUT INC.,
737 NORTH MICHIGAN AVENUE, SUITE 425, CHICAGO II, Ill., USA
LIBRARY OF CONGRESS CATALOG CARD NO. 67—17572

(C) COPYRIGHT 1967 ALEC TIRANTI LTD., LONDON W1

MADE AND PRINTED IN THE UNITED KINGDOM

CONTENTS

ACKNOWLEDGEMENTS

I am indebted to the following authorities for permission to reproduce photographs:

Aachen Cathedral. Pl. 38 (Photo, Ann Bredol-Lepper, Aachen)

The Arts Council of Great Britain. Pls. 29, 30, 37, 39 (Photo, Brompton Studio, London)

The Benaki Museum, Athens. Pls. 17, 55, 75, 76, 89, 91, 112, 113, 114, 116, 117, 118 (Photo, Benaki Museum)

The Byzantine Museum, Athens. Pls. 19-23, 44, 51, 53 (Photo, Byzantine Museum); colour plate, pls. 92, 95, 96 (Photo, M. Diamantis, Athens)

Gabinetto Fotografico Nazionale, Rome. Pls. 1-6, 50, 87, 88

Halberstadt Cathedral. Pls. 85, 86 (Photo, Mahlke Halberstadt)

The Hellenic Institute of Byzantine Studies, Venice. Pl. 18

The Institute of the History of Art, Bucharest. Pls. 35, 36, 46, 56, 57, 58, 64, 65, 68, 70, 80, 81, 82, 90, 97, 105, 106, 110 (Photo, Decorativa); pls. 79, 83, 84 (Photo, N. Ionesco)

Mansell/Alinari, London. Pl. 98

The Museum of Art, Bucharest. Pls. 15, 24, 25, 26, 27, 40, 41, 42, 45, 47, 59, 60, 61, 62, 63, 67, 69, 71, 72, 73, 74, 101, 102, 103, 104, 107, 108, 109, 111, 119, 120 (Photo, Museum of Art)

The Museum of Decorative Art, Belgrade. Pls. 66, 78, 94 (Photo, Brandibor Debeliković)

The Museum of Greek Popular Art, Athens. Pls. 28, 77 (Photo, M. Diamantis, Athens)

The Museum of the Moscow Kremlin, Palace of Arms. Pls. 7-14 (Photo, Palace of Arms)

The Victoria and Albert Museum, London. Pls. 43, 48, 54, 99, 100, 115 (Photo, V. & A. Museum)

Pl. 93 is reproduced from G. Millet, *Broderies Religieuses de Style Byzantin*, by kind permission of the Presses Universitaires de France (Photo, R. B. Fleming & Co., London)

Pls. 16, 31-34, 49, 52 are reproduced from *Clara Rhodos*, Studi e Materiali Inst. Storico Archeol. di Rodi, Vol. VII, 1933 (Photo, R. B. Fleming & Co., London)

INTRODUCTION

Sixty years ago I should have called not merely this opening chapter but the whole book An Introduction to the Byzantine Tradition in Church Embroidery. Nowadays such a title would be enough to damn the work out of hand, but that in fact is what it is. There is virtually no literature on this subject in English and little enough that could be described as available to the general reader in any other language, while so few pieces are preserved in western Europe that apart from one or two famous examples, like the so-called Dalmatic of Charlemagne in the Treasury of St. Peter's, the embroideries themselves are hardly known here. What I have tried to do is to describe in very general terms for the western reader the scope of these embroideries, what they were used for, where and how they were made, and their place in the historical and artistic background of their time. With this end in mind I have dealt with the general rather than the particular, even to the point of discussing the illustrations in relation to the whole picture rather than in precise detail. Most of the better known pieces have in fact been published, and more specific information about them is available to the student who needs it.

It might be as well to try to define here exactly which embroideries I have in mind. They were worked on vestments made for liturgical use in the Orthodox Church of the Greek rite. It is impossible to tell when they were first made, but the tradition was established during the thirteenth to the fifteenth centuries in the Constantinople of the Palaeologus emperors, and was carried on into the nineteenth century wherever the Greek Orthodox rite obtained. They were hand embroidery (as opposed to woven on a loom) in metal threads on a silk background, and with very few exceptions, they were decorated with figure subjects. The practice of embroidering Christian figures and scenes on vestments was common to both eastern and western churches in the Middle Ages, but the tradition remained unbroken in the Orthodox church, while in the west the Reformation killed the use of vestments altogether in many countries, and the purely ornamental Baroque and Rococo styles replaced the narrative embroideries in the Roman church.

Since the subject is quite large enough in any case, I have confined myself to the Greek rite and ignored the other branches of the eastern church, Coptic, Syrian, Armenian and so on. These churches did indeed use embroidered vestments, but is seems to a much lesser extent. I have also, except for a few brief references, ignored Russian church embroidery which, since the Russian church belongs to the Greek rite, should come under my heading. It is, however, a subject large enough for a book to itself, and one that I have had inadequate opportunity to study. Lastly I have only touched in passing on the very few pieces of existing embroidery which were probably of Byzantine origin but were made for western churches, and I have made no attempt to discuss Byzantine secular embroidery, for example on costume, which was almost certainly practised well before narrative embroidery on church vestments.

Of all the forms in which Byzantine religious art found expression, the embroideries are perhaps the least immediately attractive to western eyes. This is partly because embroiderers seem to have followed too closely artistic and iconographical formulae that were not of their own making. (The same of course could be said of western embroiderers of the same period, but their work gives an impression of a more adventurous attitude towards the display of the peculiar advantages of their own techniques.) Other factors which add to the difficulty are a preoccupation with liturgical conceptions which are foreign to western practice, and an insistence on a technical style which depended on subtleties of light and colour too easily blurred by the dust of passing years. So it is that the western observer falls at once under the spell of the flowing lines and pellucid colours of the mosaics of St. Saviour in Chora, but must search through greater knowledge for the same harmony of line and tone in the Salonica epitaphios.

I have therefore been in something of a quandary with regard to the background of Byzantine art and history which is a necessary launching pad for any understanding of this subject. This is clearly not the place, even if I had the knowledge, to embark on yet another history of Byzantine art, but on the other hand without some explanation the rest of the book will hardly make sense at all to the reader who is not well versed in

viii

these matters. I have therefore tried to compress the bare bones of the subject into the briefest possible space, and would urge the Byzantine historian to skip Chapter I. It does nothing but recapitulate what he has already told me.

★   ★   ★   ★   ★

Many friends have helped me in the preparation of this book, and I would like to thank them all warmly, even though it is impossible to mention them all by name.

I am particularly grateful to the Government of the Rumanian Socialist Republic, whose kind invitation enabled me to visit the magnificent collections of the Rumanian monasteries; to the Institute of the History of Art, Bucharest, and the Museum of Art, Bucharest, for their great generosity in supplying photographs, and to Mrs. Corina Nicolescu and Mrs. Viorica Dene of this Museum; to the Byzantine and Benaki Museums in Athens for photographs of pieces in their collections, and especially to Mrs. Eugenia Hadjidakis of the Benaki Museum, on whose wide knowledge of post-Byzantine embroidery in Greece I have drawn shamelessly; to Mrs. Frances Bebis of the British Council in Athens, who has taken so much trouble over my affairs; to Miss Dobrila Stojanović of the Museum of Decorative Art in Belgrade; and to Mr. Donald King of the Victoria and Albert Museum for much interest and encouragement.

I should also like to thank the staff of the Library at the Victoria and Albert Museum for their consistent helpfulness.

Above all, my gratitude is due to my husband, without whose talents as a translator from all the relevant languages I could not have studied much of the necessary literature, and whose endlessly patient explanations and criticism have enabled me to write the book at all.

PAULINE JOHNSTONE.

x

CHAPTER ONE

THE BYZANTINE BACKGROUND

The empire and civilisation known as Byzantine or East Roman sprang from the decision of Constantine I to move the imperial capital in 330 A.D. from Rome to the little town of Byzantium on the Bosphorus, which he rebuilt and renamed Constantinople. The empire met its end over a thousand years later when that great city fell to the Turks in 1453. The civilisation which it had engendered continued as a lasting influence throughout east and south-east Europe for at least another four hundred years, and in some respects remains an influence still.

During the whole of its existence the empire suffered a troubled history of almost continuous war, invasion and political intrigue, attacked from the east by Persians, Arabs and Turks, first the Seljuks and later the Ottomans who were the final cause of its downfall; from the north by barbarian tribes and later by Slavs and Bulgars; and by various groups from the west, notably the leaders of the Fourth Crusade, who were supposedly its Christian allies. The extent of its territories varied enormously from one period to another, at one time comprising the whole of Asia Minor and the eastern seaboard of the Mediterranean, Greece and much of the Balkans, the whole of Italy and the south coast of Spain, and in the end reduced to little more than the territory immediately surrounding Constantinople itself.

In spite of its stormy history, the Empire nevertheless stood firm throughout the greater part of the thousand years as the leading civilisation of the western world. Constantinople was not only a capital of tremendous opulence and luxury, but also a great centre of learning. The combination of intellectual stimulation and wealthy patronage attracted the greatest artists from all quarters, while the inner spirit of the city provided that incentive to inspired creation which produced from two opposing cultures, east and west, an art of great individuality and brilliance.

A recent writer[1] has argued that the Byzantines were by no means such devoted Christians as we have hitherto been led to suppose, and that church-going was often merely a social convention, practised by courtiers and civil servants for the

[1] G. Mathew, Byzantine Aesthetics, 1963, p. 72.

I

sake of conforming to the correct image. This may be to some extent true, but the fact remains that Christianity was felt to be a real and living force in men's lives. The beliefs and dogma of the Christian religion, and its message of hope and inspiration and victory over death, were the spiritual power which for a thousand years moved the Byzantines to record with awe and an inspired tenderness the story of the earthly life of our Lord and the majesty and glory of the Christian concept which lay behind it. Whether every artist felt himself personally stirred by this message, or regarded himself merely as a craftsman doing a good job, is hardly relevant.

When the conversion of Constantine early in the fourth century, and the adoption of Christianity as the official religion of the Roman Empire, released Christians from the burden of persecution, they set out not merely to build churches but to glorify God by adorning them with every luxury civilisation could provide. Many of the techniques of architecture, and above all the use of mosaic for decorative effect, were learnt from the east, from Syria and Sassanid Persia. At this earliest stage Christian dislike of pictorial representation of the mysteries of the faith, bred partly by reverence and partly by the necessity for secrecy in the days of persecution, combined with an eastern leaning towards pure ornament to produce a decorative style which was composed of abstract design and of symbols inherited from the days of the catacombs.

Towards the end of the century, however, the idea of teaching Christianity by pictorial means took shape, and from that time on the churches themselves and all the objects used in the celebration of the mass were decorated with scenes from the Old and New Testaments.

Art historians commonly agree that the artistic achievement of Byzantium flowered into perfect fulfilment in three separate periods during the Empire's long history. The first of these covers the latter half of the fifth and the whole of the sixth centuries, a timespan which includes the reign of the great Justinian from 527 to 565.

Extreme reverence for the throne in Sassanid Persia had led to the establishment there of a court dress and ceremonial of awe-inspiring magnificence which had had its influence in the Roman Empire as early as the reign of Diocletian (284-305). In Persian art the same attitude led to the representation of kings and their ministers in a style that was severely stylistic, rigid and heavily decorated, and this monumental manner pervaded the entire art of the Middle East, in particular the religious art of Christian Syria, providing a direct contrast to the naturalistic and oversophisticated pastoral art of the Greek city of Alexandria. It was the creative spirit of Constantinople which from the fifth century united these inharmonious elements in an entity which could truly be called Byzantine.

The church, intent on emphasising spiritual values at the expense of physical beauty, accepted more readily than secular artists the stark realistic attitudes of eastern figure drawing, which gave to Byzantine art throughout the following centuries the heavily draped, two-dimensional form which was the antithesis of the classical preoccupation with bodily perfection. From the same source, and for the same reason, came the traditional emphasis on the eyes in religious portraiture, underlining the divine nature of the subject in contrast to the carnal sensuality expressed by the mouth.

The brilliance of Justinian's rule encompassed the lavish spending on the luxurious arts that his own conception of himself demanded. The happy combination of a ruler desirous of glorifying God in practical form with craftsmen at one with his mood and furnished with the methods to suit their taste produced, among many others, the great churches of Ravenna, the Church of the Holy Apostles in Constantinople, and also in the capital the greatest masterpiece of them all, the Church of the Holy Wisdom, Agia Sophia. All of these, in their architecture and in the decorative arts that went to their adornment, expressed the majesty and rich luxury which were the hallmark of the period.

The end of Justinian's long reign saw a sad decline in his powers, one result of which was a collapse of the Empire's economy. His successors were thus left in poor case to meet a series of attacks, by the Avars in the north, the Persians and later the more formidable Arabs in the east.

The seventh century therefore was a period of war and poverty and was marked by no great artistic effort. The eighth and part of the ninth centuries were taken up in the world of art by the iconoclast controversy, which in the end was to have such a far-reaching effect on Byzantine artistic style as a whole.

This famous quarrel, which tore the Empire for a century and a half, in fact went deeper than its ostensible subject: whether or no the veneration, or even the making, of a religious picture came into the category of idolatry. Beneath this question lay the determination of the court to subdue the tremendous power which the monasteries had gathered into their own hands and to divert some of the wealth accumulated by the church into the imperial exchequer.

And yet the question of the images was more than an excuse for the persecution of the monks. Many leaders of the church had felt increasingly that the extreme veneration shown to painted pictures of the Holy Family and the saints had bordered on worship of the icons themselves, while the emperors primarily concerned, Leo III and Constantine V, were in fact pious men genuinely concerned with religious reform, although the measures that they put in train led in the end to bitter and frequently violent recrimination.

If they deplored the representation in pictures of holy persons, the Isaurian emperors were by no means puritan in outlook. Many of them, in particular

3

Theophilus (829-842), shared to the full the Byzantine taste for luxury. Thus at this period artists working for the court developed a style which dealt in secular subjects or in decorative patterns of birds, animals and leaf scrolls, and found their inspiration in a return to the old naturalistic, Hellenistic manner of Alexandria.

The monks, on the other hand, immured in their monasteries, continued in the face of all prohibition to paint icons in the severe and majestic tradition of Justinian's day. These two distinct styles were to be reunited in one great artistic movement which produced the classic period of Byzantine art during the tenth and eleventh centuries.

The church finally won its battle for the restoration of the holy pictures to their position of honour in 843, although in the deeper question of the authority of state over church the victory undeniably belonged to the former.

The year 877 saw the installation on the imperial throne of the Macedonian dynasty whose emperors were to give to Byzantium during the following century a position of unequalled splendour in the world of their time. Under them and their successors of the Comnenus dynasty in the twelfth century, Constantinople remained a leading centre of the civilised world, the seat of sophisticated elegance and above all a breeding ground of letters and the arts.

True to Byzantine tradition, mosaic decoration held the lead among the visual arts. Mosaicists once again poured the mystical spirit of Christianity into pictorial decoration of the churches. The new style, which was born of the marriage of the twin arts of iconclast days, tempered with a Hellenistic grace of drapery and freedom of movement the severe and awe-inspiring mysticism of the old tradition, and found in a stylised elegance of attitude a deep serenity which touches the sublime. The monastery church of Daphni in Attica stands as its supreme monument.

This is the great period which established the formula on which later tradition, both in painting and the minor arts, was built, and since the art of this time provides at bottom the basis of all figure representation in the embroideries, it is worth stopping here to consider its elements more closely. Dalton has summed up the synthesis of the two styles, east and west, Syrian and Alexandrian, as follows: ' The Hellenistic and the Aramaean factors in Christianity were antithetic. On the one side were intelectuality and cleverness, selective composition, logical arrangement; on the other, ill-trained zeal, love of narrative for itself, acceptance of things in the order of their event. On the one side, restraint, and the desire for grace and balance; on the other, fervour, and the resolve to reach truth in emotion, however ugly the reality. On the one side pleasing artifice, on the other, sincerity, ruthless and severe. Late-Hellenistic art was accomplished and composed, but paid for refinement in shallowness; Syrian art was without academic skill, and often crude, but strongly dramatic and intense '.[2]

[2] O. M. Dalton, East Christian Art, 1925, pp. 7-8.

4

This passage emphasises the essentially sophisticated character of Hellenistic art, and therefore of one element in Byzantine art. The naturalism of the Hellenistic approach was by no means nature in the raw, but nature permeated by artistry. It was a naturalism of flowing movement, as opposed to the rigid frontal attitudes and forbidding strength of the east, but it was expressed less in terms of actual human behaviour than as a graceful arabesque, a formal composition of line and balance.

The constant interplay between the two styles was further stressed by the division of taste between the highly educated circle surrounding the imperial court, which resulted in a recurrent renewal of the Hellenistic element in Constantinople, and the earthier requirements of the people, who remained faithful to the forceful and sometimes crude monastic style.

In the domain of the arts the Macedonian and Comnene period rose to a soaring peak from the shadowed valley of iconoclasm, but politically Byzantium had reached the beginning of the end. The death in 1180 of Manuel I Comnenus, a ruler of great ability and greater ambition, left the Empire once again faced with the familiar crisis compounded of war, insurrection, intrigue and financial chaos, and this time there was to be no recovery. 1204 saw the sack of Constantinople by the barons of the Fourth Crusade and the establishment of a Latin emperor there, while the Byzantine imperial house divided into rival factions ruling in Nicaea, Trebizond and Epirus. It is true that the feudal state set up by the crusaders foundered in inefficiency after less than sixty years and that by the year 1261 the Byzantine ruler of Nicaea, Michael Palaeologus, was re-established in the imperial capital, where his house reigned for another two centuries. Nevertheless Byzantium's standing as an impregnable political force had gone for ever and the history of the Palaeologus dynasty is one long failing struggle against the irresistible advance of the Turks.

If the Empire's strength as a political and economic power was already spent, this was by no means true where letters and the arts were concerned. The period recognised as the third great age of Byzantine art, from the latter half of the thirteenth to the middle of the fifteenth century, is really a continuation of the second, for although politically these periods were divided by the disaster of the sack of Constantinople, there was no corresponding break in the continuity of artistic expression. The Constantinople of the Palaeologi held the place that she had always occupied as the centre of creative inspiration for the art of the Christian east.

In earlier centuries western Europe had absorbed freely the influence of Byzantium in the field of both fine and applied arts. Textiles, ivories, and the work of jewellers and goldsmiths had all been much sought after in the west from the earliest years. Greek artists from Byzantium travelled to the west, many of them as refugees during the iconoclast persecutions, and there produced or inspired such great works as the cathedral of Monreale in Sicily and the monastery church of Monte Cassino. During the last two centuries western Europe in its turn contributed, principally through painters working in Serbia, which was geographically more open to western influence than the rest of the Empire, something towards the increased feeling for the human emotions which was, in Byzantium as in the west, the hallmark of the fourteenth century.

But although painters of the Tuscan school can be said to have made their contribution, Byzantium's last renaissance was largely achieved by an even more marked dependence on the inspiration to natural form lent by her own great Hellenistic antecedents. The stylised grace of the Macedonian period, which was lent a certain austerity by the deeply mystical approach to Christianity, was informed by the fourteenth century with Christian compassion and alive with a more human and earthly sense of emotion. In keeping with this trend towards humanity the Gospel stories were clothed with greater detail, more figures were added and backgrounds were filled in, where once the bare facts of an episode concentrated the attention on its symbolic significance.

In the strictest sense no work of art can be described as Byzantine after the fall of Constantinople to the Turks in 1453, when the Empire ceased to exist. The Orthodox church, however, is nothing if not traditionalist, and the spirit of Byzantium lived on in ecclesiastical art, which, partly from a sense of loyalty to the great days of the past, and partly from the physical isolation brought about by the Turkish occupation of Orthodox lands, remained even truer to its Byzantine origins over the following centuries than might otherwise have been the case. When Constantinople fell, the torch was carried by the monasteries of Mount Athos, by the churches of Moldavia and Wallachia, where Turkish suzerainty was less pressing, and by the church in Russia, which was never subject to Turkish overlordship and had absorbed the Byzantine tradition from the Greek artists who built churches and painted icons in Kiev and Novgorod.

CHAPTER TWO

TEXTILES AND EMBROIDERY

When we come to consider when gold figure embroideries were first used, we meet with very great difficulties. The earliest existing pieces, an altar cloth at St. Mark's and a pair of communion veils at Halberstadt Cathedral, can be dated with a reasonable degree of certainty to the end of the twelfth century, but they are alone, and there is very little from the following century to keep them company. The great majority of the surviving pieces belong to the Palaeologus dynasty, that is after the return of the Byzantines to Constantinople in 1261, or later. Whether narrative embroidery played a great part in the decoration of churches at an earlier period remains a problem.

It is difficult to realise nowadays, when we suffer from a surfeit of patterned materials of every kind, how greatly decorated stuffs were prized in a period when they could only be obtained by highly skilled and extremely expensive processes. There is ample evidence to show that from an early date textiles ranked very high among the minor arts and were regarded as fit shrouds for the most revered relics and suitable presents for the grandest rulers, but this position of honour appears to have been accorded to woven silks rather than to embroidery.

The early church inherited from antiquity the habit of using rich materials hung on the walls or from pillars as a means of decorating and therefore honouring the the building. In the earliest years hangings and garments may have been decorated with embroidery. Small Coptic embroideries with Christian scenes worked in coloured silks exist from the seventh century. They are roundels which were more likely to have been sewn on to garments or church vestments than on to hangings. There are also small pieces of Coptic tapestry weaving with Christian figures from the sixth century, and from the same period silks from Alexandria with Christian scenes in roundels were in great demand for hangings in churches. This was the period when Byzantium discovered the secrets of producing raw silk, and from then until the end, her silk industry, which was at its height from the tenth to the twelfth centuries, produced magnificent figured stuffs. Their subjects were not necessarily specifically Christian, but they were certainly used for the decoration of churches, and they were very highly prized both at home and abroad.

7

B

Once the silk industry had become established it seems likely that embroidery took second place. That it was used for minor purposes need not be questioned. The emperors of Justinian's house developed an elaborate system of court dress, which was in part copied by the church when the form of liturgical vesture came to be established. A study of the mosaics at Ravenna suggests that at any rate part of the decoration on the garments was embroidered rather than woven, but there is no proof of this and no surviving example. On the other hand a contemporary description by Corippus of Justinian's dress says that it was decorated with his exploits and victories by means of a fine needle as well as if it had been carried out by a paintbrush.[3] The *loros* or long scarf worn by the emperors seems to have been embroidered, largely with precious stones, and constant mention is made of gems and pearls embroidered on costume.

There is ample eivdence that decorated textiles of different kinds were used both for ecclesiastical and secular purposes. As early as the fourth century Bishop Asterios of Amasia in Asia Minor was complaining that people looked like walking frescoes, and urging his flock rather tartly to carry the life of Christ in their hearts rather than on their backs.

In the sixth century Paul the Silentiary left a famous and much quoted description of the ciborium curtains in Agia Sophia, which were decorated with figures of Christ with St. Peter and St. Paul, but there is some doubt as to how they were made. The most likely answer seems to be that they were woven silk. The gold threads also appear to have been woven into the material — ' led through the web ' — and some details may have been embroidered by hand.[4] At this period also Bishop Theodoret of Cyrrhus, like Asterios before him, speaks of the miracles of Christ worked on the clothes of rich men, but since he was concerned primarily with the moral implication, he naturally does not specify the exact method by which these unsuitably ostentatious materials were decorated. It should be noted too that these references to religious scenes on secular dress all come from Asia Minor. The capital seems to have followed rather more restrained fashions. The only pictorial record of a narrative scene used on clothing is the line of figures bearing tribute, which may represent the Adoration of the Magi, shown on the bottom of the Empress Theodora's cloak at San Vitale in Ravenna.[5] Otherwise most of the materials illustrated would appear to have been figured silk.

Figures on textiles must have been banned with the icons during the period of iconoclasm, but no vestments or church hangings have survived and it is impossible to tell what they were like. Although iconoclasm is generally regarded as having lasted throughout the eighth and the first half of the ninth centuries, there was a

[3] J. Ebersolt, Les arts somptuaires de Byzance, 1923, p. 42.
[4] G. Migeon, Les arts du tissu, 1929, p. 26; G. Mathew, Byzantine Aesthetics, 1963, p. 87.
[5] J. Ebersolt, Les arts somptuaires de Byzance, 1923, pp. 72-4.

short period when the influence of the Empress Irene caused the images to be restored. In 787 a Council of Nicaea decreed that the icons were to be re-established in the churches, and specifically mentioned vestments among the suitable vehicles for the holy figures, but by the beginning of the ninth century the decree was reversed. Icons were banned again, but the gold-decorated stole which the Patriarch Nicephorus sent as a gift to Pope Leo III must have been made before this happened. We do not know, however, whether it had figures or not, or whether the decoration was embroidered or woven.

By the middle of the tenth century the Emperor Constantine VII Porphyro-genitus, who was a considerable artist in his own right and a lavish patron of the arts, is said never to have visited a church without taking a costly vestment as a present, but again we do not know what these were like, and it seems possible that many of his gifts were silks for use as hangings, rather than liturgical vestments in the true sense.

From all this and from the contemporary descriptions of court ceremonies and uniforms, it is clear that decorated stuffs of one kind and another were widely used by church and court and also by private individuals (although gold embroidery is said to have been forbidden to the latter). Unfortunately the writers to whom we owe these references were saints, princes, historians, and not necessarily equipped to explain or even to know the difference between materials woven on a loom, embroidered by hand, or painted or block-printed, and the vocabulary used by Byzantine writers to describe gold decoration on stuffs throws no light on these distinctions.

The very high regard in which Byzantine silks were held in the west led to the copying of their famous roundel patterns in gold embroidery in countries which had no silk industry of their own, or where the industry was in its infancy, a do-it-yourself method of getting the next best thing to the fashionable materials which were so much admired. Into this category come the early eleventh century *Kunigundenmantel* and the possibly later *Reitermantel* in Bamberg cathedral, as well as the twelfth century shroud of St. Lazaire at Autun Cathedral, which is thought to have been made in Spain. Although they were evidently inspired by silk design these embroideries were very considerable works in their own right. Mediterranean countries like Sicily and Spain, which could produce the raw material for themselves, developed their own silk industries based on Arabic and Byzantine experience, but northern countries relied on hand embroidery for their sumptuous stuffs and brought it to a high degree of perfection in the latter part of the Middle Ages.

What is in doubt, and so far wholly unestablished, is when the gold embroideries of the type we are studying first came to be made by the Byzantines. Their style is a distinctive one based on pictorial representation of Christian figures and scenes as they were depicted in mosaic, and on the technique of laid gold thread embroidery with some coloured silk. Diehl has described the gold embroideries of the fourteenth and fifteenth centuries as the one great extravagance which the church allowed itself in this time of poverty.[6] In the political and economic circumstances of the Empire under the Palaeologi the luxurious methods of decoration of former centuries were impossible. Although recent researches have shown that mosaic was still used in a few churches in the capital, many of the great churches of the period, in the Serb monasteries and at Mistra in the Peloponnese, were decorated in fresco. It is true that the subtler colouring and greater fluidity of line possible in fresco suited the naturalistic and humanist style of fourteenth century artists and produced masterpieces worthy to stand beside the finest of the mosaics, but the use of the medium was undoubtedly an economy measure.

It is possible, therefore, that the embroideries, although executed in gold and silver and in their own right one of the minor triumphs of Byzantine craftsmen, were thought of orginally not as an extravagance, but as a cheaper substitute for the costly woven textiles which required such a high degree of skilled workmanship. Countries such as Byzantium, Persia and Japan, which at various periods have attained a very high degree of skill in the production of decorated textiles, have always regarded embroidery very much in the light of a poor relation.

The suggestion of an economy measure seems to bear out the theory, and it must be emphasised that this is not more than a theory, that this particular *type* of embroidery did not come into being very much before the twelfth century and did not really achieve importance until the return of the house of Palaeologus to Constantinople in 1261. It must be remembered that Byzantium's economic difficulties started with the over-generous trading concessions made to Venice and Genoa by Alexius I Comnenus in the early years of the twelfth century. By the end of that century the Angelus emperors, under whose rule the Halberstadt veils were made, had by their own folly and extravagance aggravated the already serious economic troubles of the empire, and they were more given to melting down or selling the imperial treasures than to subsidising the expensive products of imperial workrooms.

There is no doubt that the period of the Palaeologus dynasty established these embroideries as the classic form of vestment in the Orthodox church for at least three hundred years to come. The difficulty is to know whether the style came into use much before their time. The Byzantines were confirmed present-givers, every visiting monarch and ambassador receiving his quota of luxuries from the imperial workshops, every accredited ambassador bearing gifts to the court he visited. By this means and from the dowries of Byzantine princesses married to

[6] C. Diehl, Manuel d'art byzantin, 1925, Vol. II, p. 738.

western nobles and from loot brought back by returning Crusaders, the cathedral treasuries of Europe have acquired and preserved a fair number of Byzantine works of art. The fact is, however, that there are very few embroideries indeed among these treasures, and this must surely point to the conclusion that in the period when Byzantium made and sent abroad gifts that were highly valued because such things did not exist in the west, there were simply no embroideries to send. By the thirteenth and fourteenth centuries, when such embroideries were undoubtedly made in Constantinople, very few were sent to the west, partly, presumably, because of the lack of sympathy between the two churches and the difference in the style of the vestments used, even more because by this time western Europe had church embroideries of its own which were at least the equal of those made in the east.

Again, even if we are to believe that everything of value in Constantinople itself was utterly destroyed, either by those emperors of the house of Angelus who melted their gold treasure through extravagance or necessity, or by the sacking of the city by Crusaders and later by the Turks, it is hardly credible that no piece of ecclesiastical embroidery should have survived had it existed. Embroidery may be perishable, and this will account for the fact that no garments have survived. It is also portable and therefore highly suitable as a gift to travellers, and yet no piece of this particular style which can be dated before the Halberstadt veils remains.

CHAPTER THREE

VESTMENTS*

The reign of the Palaeologus dynasty, that is to say from the middle of the thirteenth to the middle of the fifteenth century, coincided with the finest period for church embroidery in the west. First England and Germany, then France, the Low Countries and Italy, produced magnificent vestments and furnishings for ecclesiastical use, but owing to the difference in the rites of the two churches the objects chosen for embroidery in east and west were not always the same.

The embroidery style in the eastern church which appears to have crystallised under the Palaeologi was of course merely a form of decoration. The articles of dress worn by the priest and the various veils and hangings used in the service were nearly all established in the ritual well before the thirteenth century.

Church vestment developed naturally from the clothes in every day use during the period of the church's establishment. In the earliest years, and for secrecy during the years of persecution, the celebrant at a church service wore his everyday clothes. As most writers on vestment have pointed out, St. Paul, when he asked Timothy to bring his cloak from Troas, was not asking for a cope but for the overcoat he had left behind.

When the fourth century brought freedom from persecution, some synods began to insist on formality in dress for the officiating clergy. As frequently happened in later centuries, formality meant the rejection of innovation and adherence to a style beginning to die out, much as morning dress is nowadays worn for formal occasions although it is entirely outmoded in everyday life. In this way dress that became traditional for the clergy was based on Roman dress of the third and fourth centuries, although some time elapsed before the secular garment came to be regarded without any doubt as a liturgical vestment, worn specially for the celebration of the mass. This development occurred later with some vestments than others and at different times in different places. There was, of course, no formal division in the church until the eleventh century, and

*A short list of vestments is given at Appendix I for easy reference.

12

vestment in east and west developed roughly along the same lines, and in fact remains basically the same in its final development in the two churches in spite of minor differences.

In a slightly different category were those articles of vestment which were not so much garments as insignia. These were originally the stole for priest and deacon, and the bishop's pallium. It would appear that these two items, and later the maniple, were never practical items of dress or equipment but were created from the outset as distinguishing marks of the clergy. Their history goes back to the fourth century in the Greek church, and their use spread to the west over the next two hundred years.

As the centuries passed the mundane origins of vestment in ordinary clothes were forgotten, and a symbolic religious significance was attached to various items, usually as a result of writings by early commentators on the meanings of the liturgy and church practice. A given article can therefore have a ' real ' provenance based on historic fact, and a traditional symbolic one, which served to increase its sanctity in the eyes of the beholder. This was particularly true in the eastern church, where a strong strain of mysticism encouraged a leaning towards symbolism.

Symbolic meanings attached to vestments in the west tended to be moral labels, such as love, chastity, humility, and changed more often through the centuries according to different interpreters. The western mystics of the twelfth century did turn for a time to the Greek conception of the bishop as Christ's representative, dressed in His garments. The first Greek writing to express this idea is the *Istoria Ekklesiastiki,* a document which is thought to have been written by a monk some time before the ninth century. The identification of various vestments with the garments and trappings of the Crucifixion, the purple robe, the reed put into Christ's hand, the fetters which bound Him, the Cross He carried and so on, was repeated and sometimes added to by later Greek liturgical writers until it became part of a fixed tradition which has endured in the Greek rite until modern times.

The Orthodox church makes a clear distinction between the *hierarchical* and the *liturgical* vestments, that is to say those worn by the priest, and those used for the adornment of the altar and the church. The first category can be further divided into the actual garments of the priest and the insignia of his office.

THE HIERARCHICAL VESTMENTS *

Sticharion and Epimanikia

The under vestment in both churches was the long tunic which was worn by everyone under the Roman and early Byzantine empires and corresponded to the

*Much of the information on the origins and symbolic meanings of vestments contained in the sections on Hierarchical Vestment and the Priestly Insignia is derived from J. Braun, Die liturgische Gewandung, Freiburg, 1907.

13

chiton of classical Greece. This became the alb in the western church and the sticharion in the eastern.

The sticharion of a bishop was decorated with the *clavi* inherited from the dress of the Roman consuls. These were two narrow bands of red ornament from shoulder to hem known to the Greeks as *potamoi* (rivers). They were described in the *Istoria Ekklesiastiki* as representing the blood flowing from the Saviour's side. More important to the student of embroidery were the bands of ornament decorating the narrow sleeves of the early sticharion, and described by the same source as the manacles that were put on Christ when He was bound and taken from the Chief Priest to Pilate.

As the decoration became more elaborate it was no longer worked on the sleeves of the sticharion itself, but on a separate pair of detachable cuffs, the *epimanikia*. These were worn in the Greek church only by bishops, but they should not be confused with the gloves worn by bishops in the west. There is in fact no parallel vestment in the west.

There is no fixed subject for the embroidery, but the Annunciation was often chosen, sometimes with the angel on one cuff and the Virgin on the other, sometimes with the whole scene on both.

Phelonion

The vestment worn over the sticharion was simply the round cloak, with a hole for the head but no other opening, which was worn as a bad weather garment by all classes under the Roman empire. It was called *paenula* in Latin and *phainoles* or *phailonion* in Greek. This developed in the western church into both chasuble and cope, but in the Greek rite it remained one garment, the *phelonion*, and is worn by the priest for all ceremonies, not only for the celebration of the mass. In both churches it had come to be recognised as a specifically liturgical garment, rather than an item of clothing, by the seventh century.

In fact the Greek phelonion is precisely the same garment as the medieval bell chasuble in the west. The fashion for cutting away the sides of the chasuble to make it more wearable for the celebrant, which was started in the fourteenth century in the west, had no parallel until after the middle ages, probably as late as the sixteenth century, in the east. It was first gathered up and later cut shorter in the front to free the priest's arms.

The phelonion, which in the middle ages was white for festal seasons and dark red or purple for seasons of fasting, was never used for a display of embroidery, as were both cope and chasuble in the west, but from the eleventh century the white phelonion of a patriarch began to be decorated all over with crosses and was called *polystavrion* (lit. with many crosses). By the end of the twelfth century, Balsamon, Patriarch of Antioch, still insisted that the polystavrion was a patriarchal right, but by the fourteenth century it was worn by the metropolitans, and later by all bishops. This vestment is constantly illustrated in medieval frescoes, icons and miniatures, and even in embroidery, but no actual example from Byzantine times appears to have survived.

A modern form of phelonion worn in the Armenian and Syrian churches is cut down the front like a cope, and so is a cloak (*mandyas*) worn by bishops of the Greek church, but this last is not a liturgical vestment. These sometimes have applied medallions of embroidery on the lower corners of the opening, which are said to represent the writing of Old and New Testaments. There is in fact no vestment in the eastern churches which is strictly comparable to the cope.

Saccos

The saccos, which in the middle ages was the ceremonial vestment of certain privileged patriarchs, was a tunic with short wide sleeves which was originally an imperial garment. Its use appears to have been granted in the first place to selected patriarchs as a sign of imperial favour. The first literary reference is again in Balsamon, and by the thirteenth century it was worn not only by all patriarchs but also by some metropolitans, although only for the feasts of Christmas, Easter and Whitsun. After the fall of Constantinople it began to be worn by all bishops and replaced the polystavrion. Traditionally it was said to represent the purple cloak put on Christ by His tormentors.

Embroidery on a saccos can be very elaborate, although there is no set subject. The most famous and earliest existing example is the fourteenth century saccos in the Vatican known as the Dalmatic of Charlemagne, and there are other Byzantine 1-6
sacci in Moscow, two of which, made for the Metropolitan Photius early in the 7-14
fifteenth century, are particularly fine. Late examples are fairly common.

Mitre

The mitre in both churches is of relatively late origin. In the west it derived from a cap-like headdress worn by the Pope outside church services, and was first accepted as a liturgical vestment about the middle of the tenth century in Rome and later elsewhere. In the Greek church the celebration of the liturgy in any form of headdress was a privilege peculiar to the Patriarch of Alexandria until a very late date, but when or why the custom should have arisen there is obscure. It certainly dates to the tenth century. It is clear, however, from Byzantine writers on liturgical dress that only Alexandria and no other Greek bishop wore a headdress up to the early years of the fifteenth century. It is possible that the mitre came into general use for bishops after the fall of Constantinople. It was certainly worn by at any rate some of the Greek bishops during the sixteenth century, and was introduced into Russia when the Patriarchate was established there in 1589.

There are three kinds of Greek mitre, of which the first is the most interesting as regards embroidery. This is the earliest type, and is simply a round, flat-topped cap derived from a monastic headdress. It was embroidered with a scene on the top and scenes or figures in arcaded sections round the sides.

The other two types were very similar and were copied from the Byzantine imperial crown and the headdress of high Byzantine officials, probably to recall to the people after the fall of Byzantium to the Turks, that the sacred authority of the emperor, who had been regarded as God's representative on earth, lived on in the head of the church. Both are high and rounded, and one has the crossed bands of the imperial crown, surmounted by a cross. They are made of stiffened material and precious metals, ornamented with stones or enamel plaques, but seldom with embroidery of the type we are discussing.

Mirković describes and illustrates two embroidered mitres made for Serb metropolitans, one in the fifteenth and one in the sixteenth century.[7] These are beehive-like in shape, with an upstanding cross on top. The earlier one must have been made at about the time the mitre first came into general use among bishops, although there is nothing to show whether it was a liturgical headdress in the strict sense or merely for processional wear outside the church.

THE PRIESTLY INSIGNIA

We come now to those vestments which were not derived from garments in every-day use, but which, according to Braun,[8] were designed from the outset to provide distinguishing insignia for the clergy. These were the *omophorion* for a bishop (the western pallium) and the *epitrachilion* and *orarion* for priest and deacon respectively (the western stola). Both omophorion and stole date back to the fourth century in the eastern church, and to about the fifth in the west. Later we find in both churches a ceremonial cloth which became the *epigonation*, hanging from the girdle, in the east, and the maniple, hanging from the wrist, in the west. All have been used as vehicles for lavish embroidery in both churches.

Epitrachilion and Orarion

Both the stole, which distinguished the higher ranks of the clergy from the lower, and the omophorion worn by the bishop appear to have originated in some form of cloth, towel or scarf, but from the time of its origin the cloth was carried as a sign of rank and not with any practical purpose. It was the folding of the cloth into a strip which produced the long narrow stole which we know.

The first mention of the stole in the eastern church is found in the middle of the fourth century in a ruling of the Council of Laodicea which, since it gives sub-deacons the right to wear the stole but denies it to lectors and cantors, seems to indicate that the vestment was already in use at that time as a distinguishing mark of the higher ranks, that is ordained priests and deacons. It was first mentioned as a liturgical vestment in the west during the sixth century.

[7] Mirković, Crkveni Umetnički Vez, p. 36, pl. XVII.
[8] Braun, op. cit., p. 618.

16

During this early period the universal name for the stole was *orarion* or *orarium*. About the ninth century a distinction came to be made in the Greek rite between the priest's stole and the deacon's. The latter continued to be called orarion, while the stole worn by the priest was called epitrachilion. It was presumably also at this time or during the following century that the two halves of the epitrachilion, which was wider than the orarion, were joined throughout their length in front as they hung round the wearer's neck. At a later date the neck was made narrower than the rest of the stole and shaped into a collar which could be slipped over the head. The deacon's stole remained one long strip and was worn over the left shoulder. In the west at about the same period the word *stola* came to be used instead of orarium, but the practice of crossing the ends over the breast prevented them from being joined. No distinction was made between the stole of priest and deacon.

Various symbolic meanings have been given to the two stoles in the Greek church. One authority refers to the epitrachilion as the rope which was tied round the Saviour's neck when He was led to His trial, just as the epimanikia were compared with the fetters on His wrists. (Matthew 27, 2. ' And when they had bound him they led him away and delivered him to Pontius Pilate '.) The right side of the stole was said to represent the reed placed in His hand by the soldiers who mocked Him, and the left the Cross He was compelled to carry on His shoulders.

A fifth century writer, Isidore of Pelusium, refers to a linen cloth carried by the deacons as a sign of office. This was said to represent the cloth used by the Saviour in the Washing of Feet, and was thus symbolic of Christ's role as servant of His people and of the similar role of the deacon as servant of the church. This cloth (*othoni*) has been equated by some authorities with the epigonation and by others with the orarion, both of which originated as a ceremonial cloth or hand-kerchief. Since, however, the orarion was the insignia of the deacon and the epigonation was not in use in Isidore's time, it seems clear that the analogy was originally applied to the former.

Another writer of the same period describes deacons as equipped for their office with a linen cloth over the shoulder in imitation of the winged angels. This comparison of the role of the deacons in the church with that of the angels in heaven appears to have caught the imagination of liturgical writers and became an established tradition. Deacons as angels are illustrated in a miniature of the Menologion of Basil II,[9] where their clothing is swept back over the shoulders to indicate wings. Angels as deacons became an accepted iconographical feature, indicating the heavenly servitor.

The first decorated stole to be mentioned is the one already referred to which

[9] Vatican Library, late tenth cent. Illus., Ebersolt, Les arts somptuaires, p. 29.

17

was sent to Pope Leo III early in the ninth century, but there is no means of telling what the decoration was like.[10] No surviving epitrachilion can be dated earlier than the late fourteenth century. From that time the vestment was usually resplendently embroidered, even though it was worn under the phelonion and most of its length was therefore hidden from sight. The stole in the west, which was likewise worn under the chasuble, was usually only decorated on the ends for this reason. The traditional decoration on an epitrachilion divided the length by one device or another into sections which framed the figures of Prophets, Apostles, Saints or Fathers of the Church, or sometimes the scenes which marked the Great Feasts. From the fifteenth century, when the sections were usually marked by architectural arcading, the arrangement of the epitrachilion can be compared with the orphrey on the western cope.

In the late middle ages the parallel drawn between deacons and angels was responsible for the use of the thrice-repeated Holy of the Sanctus, the angelic hymn of praise, as decoration for the orarion. The words ἅγιος, ἅγιος, ἅγιος are shown written vertically on the oraria of the deacon/angels in fourteenth century embroideries. They are sometimes used vertically on actual surviving oraria, and sometimes horizontally as bands of decoration are used on an epitrachilion. Oraria were also traditionally decorated with angels and cherubim.

Omophorion

The omophorion, which was the distinguishing sign of a bishop, was used in this way, like the stole, as early as the fourth century. It probably had its origin in a ceremonial scarf, and later became a long strip of material laid across the shoulders with one end falling in front and the other behind. The western pallium is the same vestment.

Its symbolic meaning is also attributed to Isidore of Pelusium, who describes it as the sheep carried on the shoulders of the Good Shepherd, indicating the bishop's role as shepherd of his flock. In early centuries, and at any rate until about 1400, it was always made of wool, but later came to be made of silk.

An omophorion is traditionally decorated with five crosses or circles (*poloi*), one at each end, one on each shoulder and one on the neck. In addition it has bands of decoration on the ends called, like the bands on the sticharion, *potamoi* (rivers). All these were embroidered separately and applied to the vestment. The crosses were large enough to carry a scene in the centre with saints or cherubim in the arms.

Epigonation

The vestment now known as epigonation is worn only in the Greek and Armenian churches. It was earlier called *encheirion* (a hand cloth). According to Braun,

[10] Braun, op. cit., p. 592.

18

both this and the cloth which developed into the western maniple came into use about the eighth or ninth centuries.[11] The cloth originated as a towel or hand-kerchief, but in a strictly formal and ceremonial sense. In the Greek church its use was, and is, confined to bishops. It is illustrated in manuscript and mosaic from the eleventh century onwards as a folded cloth hanging from the arm or tucked into the girdle on the right side. (The western maniple is worn on the left arm.)

Towards the end of the twelfth century Balsamon refers to it as epigonation, which seems to indicate that by his time it had already assumed its modern form, that is to say the square of material is stiffened so that the decoration can be displayed, and it is suspended from the girdle by one corner to hang at about knee height, presumably so that it can be seen below the phelonion. Hence the name epigonation (lit. knee piece). It has nothing to do with kneeling.

Symbolically the epigonation is said to stand for the Sword of the Spirit, which appears to belong to a conception of the vested bishop as the Christian warrior clad in the Armour of God, rather than the traditional analogy with Christ sacrificed. Various scenes have been used to decorate the vestment. The Anastasis is common on early examples, and later the Transfiguration. The Washing of Feet was also used occasionally, which suggests that later liturgical writers related the epigonation to the *othoni* mentioned by Isidor of Pelusium. As the square was hung by one corner it presented a diamond shape, and embroidery is usually so placed that it is seen correctly at this angle.

This completes the list of vestments actually worn by the priest, as garments or insignia. A clear picture of a bishop fully vested is shown in the icon of St. Dionysius the Areopagite, and in the representation of Christ on the Chilandari curtain.[12]

THE LITURGICAL VESTMENTS

The liturgical vestments most often met with in embroidery are the veils used to cover the Sacred Elements and the processional veil which is a development of the largest of these, the *Epitaphios Sindon*. Various veils used to decorate the sanctuary and the curtain for the door of the iconostasis, as well as the cloth used to adorn an icon, also come into this category.

The eastern custom of using draperies of all kinds as decoration was adopted by the Christian church at a very early date. Curtains and hangings of rich stuffs were part of the normal furnishing of a church, as we can see from contemporary descriptions of Agia Sophia and from illustrations in early manuscripts. They must also have been used in palaces and private houses. Decorative cloths are

[11] Braun, op. cit., p. 551.
[12] Millet, Broderies, pl. CLIX.

still used in this way in peasant houses in Greece.

A much later description, from the beginning of the fifteenth century, has been left by a chronicler of the Council of Constance, Ulrich von Richental,[13] who describes the eager curiosity with which the Latins watched the arrangements made by the Russian delegation to celebrate the Orthodox Liturgy in a room set aside for them to use as a chapel. He speaks of the gold cloth covering chalice and patten as being 'als wyt und als brait, als ein halby elen' (as wide and as broad as half an ell), and in a long description mentions at least half a dozen 'gold cloths' hung round the room and the table to be used for the celebration. The Russians, of course, were transforming an ordinary room into a chapel, and perhaps used more hangings on that account, but in general the principle of using decorative veils in the sanctuary seems to have held good right through the fourteenth century and later.

As soon as the celebration of the Eucharist developed from its earliest form when it was simply a gathering in a private house, it became necessary to segregate the celebrants from the congregation, and this was done at first by a low partition of marble. Later, pillars were added to the barrier, and curtains hung between them.

One of the essential differences between the Eastern Liturgy and the Western Mass lies in the deeply mystic approach of the Orthodox mind, compared to the more objective and realistic attitude of the west, a difference which has its roots in the very nature of the peoples concerned. Orthodox mysticism regarded the most sacred moments of the Liturgy as too holy to be exposed to public view. This attitude to the veiled altar is summed up by St. John Chrysostom:[14]

'And if thou believest not, look to this table, call to mind for whose sake it is set, and why; consider who it is that is coming forth here, tremble with awe even before the time. For so, when one sees the throne only of a king, in heart he rises up, expecting the king's coming forth. And do thou accordingly thrill with awe even before that thrilling moment; raise up thyself, and before thou seest the veils drawn aside and the choir of angels marching forth, ascend thou to the very heaven'.

The Roman west, on the other hand, insisted that the whole of the Mass should be performed in full view of the congregation, so that all might participate. The dividing screen and curtains for the altar are mentioned by eastern writers as early as the fourth century, long before any curtain was used in the west.[15]

[13] R. M. Buck, Ulrich von Richentals Chronik der Conzil von Constanz, Bibliotek des litterärischen Vereins in Stuttgart, 1882.

[14] Homilies of St. J. Chrysostom on I Corinthians, No. 36, trs. Cornish and Medley, A Library of the Fathers (ed. Pusey), 1838.

[15] J. Braun, Der christliche Altar, Vol. II, p. 275.

The Orthodox sanctuary therefore has always been shielded from the public gaze. When the Holy Table was moved from the centre to the apse of the basilica, the dividing screen, still consisting of a low partition or rails and low pillars with curtains, was used to cut off the apse from the rest of the church and thus form the sanctuary. In the Orthodox church this 'altar space' which is called *vima* (lit. the platform or tribune) is equated with the Judgment Throne.

From the fourth century, especially in large churches, a ciborium was sometimes used as protection for the Table, and this too had curtains hanging between the pillars, either on all four sides or on the side facing the congregation. It was these curtains in Agia Sophia which were the subject of the famous description by Paul the Silentiary. The curtain on the front side of the altar was said to represent the veil of the Jewish temple. Later, at any rate by the eighth century, the sanctuary was always hidden by a screen, which eventually became higher and more elaborately decorated and was used to display a series of holy pictures. The high iconostasis dates at the earliest from the fifteenth century, and in some areas, Moldavia among them, was not known until the end of the sixteenth, but it is part of every Orthodox church today. The earlier partition or rails was not called iconostasis.

It was never intended, however, to exclude the congregation entirely from the celebration by the priest, and curtains or veils which could be open or closed at various times in the service were always a feature of the screen. The true iconostasis, which was of solid wood or marble, was and is pierced by three pairs of doors, of which the central pair, or Royal Doors, were much lower than the screen itself. The space above them was filled by a richly decorated curtain, which necessarily grew longer as the screen grew higher.

A series of embroidered curtains or hangings therefore existed, which were used to decorate the walls of the sanctuary itself, to hang between the pillars of the ciborium or between the pillars or over the door in the low screen, or over the door in the later high iconostasis. At this distance of time it is not always possible to distinguish the exact use to which these hangings were put. Some were clearly intended for a specific saint's day or festival, particularly for a church dedicated to the saint concerned. Two hangings of the Dormition at Putna and one of the **57** Three Hierarchs from Jassy come into this category.[16]

Alternatively the curtains were decorated with scenes reflecting the symbolic meaning of the Liturgy. The famous curtain of Euphemia at Chilandari[17] shows Christ arrayed as a bishop, that is as the Celebrant, and attended by St. Basil and St. Gregory Nazianzene as deacons. From the sixteenth century the Crucifixion was a very usual subject.

[16] A. R. P. R. Studii, p. 166, fig. 18.
[17] Millet, Broderies, pl. CLIX.

In the same category as these decorative veils is another called the *podea*, which was used to adorn, and therefore to do honour to, an icon.[18] This custom, of course, also had its origins in the tradition of using valuable stuffs as decoration The top of the holy picture was draped with the *mandylion* (handkerchief) while the podea hung below it. The earliest references to the use of podeai are found in eleventh century writings and inventories. The word actually means the hem or border of a garment or cover. Thus a sermon of this period described an icon showing a half-length portrait of the Virgin Hodigitria, of which the podea was represented as covering her feet, that is as the lower half of her dress. In this way the faithful could benefit by touching the hem of her garment. In the same way the podea of the famous icon of Christ of the Khalki was described as recalling the story of the woman diseased with an issue of blood, who was cured by touching the hem of the Saviour's garment. (Matthew 9, 20-22.) It was also said that Alexius I Comnenus had been miraculously cured by being wrapped in this podea.

A podea belonged to a particular icon, was consecrated in its honour and sometimes presented as a thank offering to the saint it represented. Inventories indicate that different podeai might be kept for everyday and feast days.

A podea could be any kind of decorated cloth, but we are concerned here with those embroidered with a figure subject, of which the earliest examples date from the fifteenth century. The subject chosen was always connected with the icon for which the cloth was intended, but it was not a copy of the icon. It is a curious fact that so few podeai of the Virgin and Child exist, in view of the enormous number of icons painted of this subject. A sixteenth century example made for the Virgin of Tikhvin in Suzdal, and now in the Tretyakov Gallery in Moscow, is one of the few instances of a Virgin and Child carried out in embroidery. In fact the custom of using an embroidered podea seems to have been particularly prevalent in Russia and to have continued until a later date there than elsewhere.

Some podeai have been described as being themselves embroidered icons, rather than decorative additions for a painting, but if some of the cloths were so intended, it seems to be almost impossible to distinguish them. Nor is it easy to tell if a large cloth was meant as a decorative veil for the sanctuary or as a podea for a large icon in the iconostasis or on the *proskynitaria*, that is the desk used to display a special icon in the nave of the church. Some writers consider the later of the two Dormitions at Putna to have been a podea.

The podea has fallen almost entirely into disuse, at any rate in the sense that its decoration was intended to complement a particular icon. Embroidered cloths of one kind and another are still used in a church to cover the *proskynitaria*, or sometimes in a private house to drape the top of a revered holy picture.

[18] For a detailed discussion of the subject, see A. Frolov, La podéa, in Byzantion, Vol. 13, 1938.

The early history and development of coverings for the altar and Sacred Elements is confused by the fact that the names and exact uses of the different cloths changed and interchanged over the centuries. The altar was covered from a very early date with a linen cloth, symbolising the linen in which the Body of Christ was wrapped. At any rate from the end of the fourth century this was covered by another cloth, richer in material and decoration, called the *endyti*. A later symbolic interpretation by Simeon of Salonica (late fourteenth century) recalls the 93rd Psalm, The Lord is King and has put on Glorious Apparel, and maintains that the linen represented the Body of Christ and the endyti His covering of Glory.[19]

The endyti could be said to correspond to the western frontal, but it covered the top and all four sides of the Holy Table. Owing to the much smaller size and square shape of the Orthodox altar and its position in the middle of the sanctuary instead of against a wall, no vestment which is really the equivalent of an altar frontal exists in the eastern church. The few 'frontals' in the west which are of Byzantine workmanship must either have been executed as a special commission for a Catholic church or, if ever intended for use in an Orthodox church, have been designed as hangings for the sanctuary wall.

The endyti is and always has been of rich material and decorated in some way, but strangely it does not seem to have been used as a vehicle for narrative embroidery, unlike the frontal, which provided some of the finest pieces of medieval embroidery in the west. Three altar coverings recorded in Ravenna in the sixth century are said to have been decorated with the figure of Christ with four others, with scenes from His Life, and with bishops of Ravenna, but there is the usual difficulty in knowing whether they were embroidered or woven.[20] Representations of the vested altar in mosaic and miniature painting and in embroidery itself never show figure subjects on the endyti but only abstract designs. Three miniatures in the Menologion of Basil II (976-1025)[21] show altar cloths with, respectively, an all-over lattice pattern, decorative crosses, and the so-called *gammadia* in the corners and a cross in the middle. This last design, which had a right-angled or L-shaped decoration (in Greek the capital letter gamma — hence the name) applied in the four corners on the front of the cloth, appears to have been very widespread, and is frequently reproduced in embroidery, as for example in the Communion of the Apostles on the Vatican saccos. Whether these representations show abstract decoration simply from a desire to avoid pictures within a picture, or because in fact the endyti was decorated as they show it, it is impossible

[19] G. Sotiriou, Τὰ λειτουργικὰ ἄμφια in θεολογία, κ, Athens, 1949, p. 605.
[20] J. Braun, Der christliche Altar, Vol. II, p. 51.
[21] J. Braun, op. cit., pls. 146, 151, 116.

to tell, but the latter explanation seems more likely.

Simeon of Salonica describes a veil decorated with the Four Evangelists which has been identified by one writer with the endyti,[22] but the passage is not at all clear[23] and it seems more likely that he was referring to a ciborium veil. No actual endyti from Byzantine times appears to have survived.

In the Byzantine period another cloth called *eiliton* (lit. that which is rolled up) was laid on the altar over the endyti so that the Sacred Vessels stood on it. This, like the linen cloth, was also likened by the Early Fathers to the linen in which the Body of Christ was wrapped, and in fact it is the equivalent of the Latin corporal. Another reference in the writings of Simeon indicate that in his time it was decorated with a cross, or with the Body of Christ and angels with fans, but, as in the case of the endyti, no piece has survived which has been identified as an eiliton. After the Turkish conquest its use died out in the Orthodox church except as a wrapping for another consecrated cloth, the *antiminsion*.

The antiminsion was originally a portable altar used in the period of persecution, when it might be necessary to move at a moment's notice. After the official acceptance of Christianity it was still used as a portable altar on occasions when the Liturgy was celebrated where there was no church, perhaps for armies in the field or for travellers. Strictly speaking it was only an altar covering in the sense that it was a consecrated cloth used to transform whatever makeshift table was to hand — in other words it was itself the altar. It was not at first intended for use on a consecrated altar in a church, but from the fourteenth century came to be used on every altar in place of the eiliton.

Most writers have considered that the medieval antiminsion was embroidered, but Ştefanescu has put forward the theory that this was never so, and that it was always painted or printed.[24] This seems reasonable when it is considered that raised embroidery could overturn the chalice or catch falling crumbs of the Host in its threads. The modern antiminsion is undoubtedly always printed. An antiminsion is consecrated by a bishop, whose signature it bears, and carries holy relics in a small pocket stitched on the back.

Ştefanescu lists a number of painted antiminsia, the earliest being a Russian example dated 1149.[25] The earliest decoration seems to have been simply a cross with the monogram IC XC NIKA (Jesus Christ conquers) and an inscription. Later the Lance and Sponge were added and the symbols of the Evangelists. (The names of the Four Evangelists, regarded as the founders of the church, were

[22] G. Sotiriou, loc. cit.
[23] Ştefanescu, Voiles, p. 102.
[24] I. D. Ştefanescu, Autels, tissus et broderies liturgiques, in Analecta, Universitatea din Bucureşti, II, 1944, p. 113.
[25] Ştefanescu, op. cit., pp. 111ff.

written on the corners of the altar itself.) From the last years of the sixteenth century figure subjects are found on the antiminsion. Christ rising from a sarcophagus was used frequently during the seventeenth century. Eventually the Lamentation was introduced and the decoration of an antiminsion became identical with that of the epitaphios, which is discussed at the end of this chapter.

The liturgical vestments that are most frequently met with in embroidery are the veils used to cover chalice and patten on the altar, and their close relation, perhaps descendant would be a better word, the *epitaphios sindon*.

The Communion Vessels were covered separately by veils called the Little Aëres and together by the Great Aër. The little aëres were also called respectively *diskokalymmata* (for the patten) and *potirokalymmata* (for the chalice). Although small compared with the Great Aër they are often considerably larger than similar veils in the western church. Quite a number of embroidered examples survive from the Middle Ages, nearly all decorated with the Communion of the Apostles, shown in each kind on the appropriate veil of a pair. From the sixteenth century the Christ Child in the Patten was also used frequently. The modern chalice veil is in the form of a cross when laid flat: the four arms fold down to make a box-shaped cover for the chalice instead of a draped cloth.

The history of the Great Aër is much more complicated, since its use changed with changes in the Liturgy, especially during the fourteenth century when the ritual was enlarged and enriched. In its very earliest form the aër was connected with the fans used by the deacons to keep the flies from the Sacred Elements, and may even itself have been a fan of peacock's feathers. A prayer from the Liturgy of St. James,[26] the εὐχὴ τοῦ καταπετάσματος (prayer of the curtain), has led to a certain amount of confusion, since the word *katapetasma* usually indicated a curtain, whether on the ciborium or iconostasis, while this prayer clearly refers to the aër, which was used to cover or reveal the Sacred Vessels at different times in the service and was waved as a fan over the celebrant's head during the Creed.

Certainly by the fourteenth century decoration on the great aër had become established. It consisted of the Body of the Crucified Christ laid on the Red Stone of Ephesus, and symbolising, in this case, the mystical change in the Bread and Wine which it covered. The Christ was guarded by angels carrying fans, and the Evangelists or their symbols appeared in the corners. This iconography was based on the wording and symbolic meaning of the Liturgy, and will be considered at greater length in Chapter IV. It was also an exact parallel of the decoration of the antiminsion.

At this period the Great Aër was carried in the procession known as the Great

[26] The Liturgy of St. James was used from at least the fourth century in the Jacobite Rite, based on Antioch. It is one of the Liturgies used on rare occasions in the Orthodox rite.

Entry when the Gifts of Bread and Wine were brought to the Holy Table for consecration. The aër was in fact carried on the heads of the clergy taking part, a scene which is clearly illustrated in frescoes in the Lavra monastery on Mount Athos, at Mistra and at Kaisariani near Athens. It also began to play a special role in the Good Friday services. It was used to wrap the Book of the Four Gospels, which was carried on the priest's shoulder to symbolise the Body of Christ wrapped in the shroud provided by St. Joseph of Arimathea. Later the veil itself, already adorned with a representation of the mystical Body of Christ, was carried in the Good Friday procession to represent the actual Body of Christ the Man. It was in this capacity that it was known as the *Epitaphios Sindon* (lit. the sepulchral linen).[27]

In point of fact the processional aër is usually called epitaphios as well, and it is therefore important to make the distinction between the *liturgical* epitaphios, which was a processional veil iconographically linked with the celebration of the Communion, and the *Good Friday* epitaphios, which was also used in procession but specifically related to mourning for the Crucifixion. The liturgical epitaphios was already distinct from the great aër in that it was too big and heavy to be used as a covering for the altar vessels. It was either laid on the altar after the Great Entry or hung on the walls of the sanctuary. The change in function took place gradually towards the end of the fourteenth century. An element of mourning had already been introduced into the iconography by weeping angels quite early in this century. The Nicholas Eudaimonoioannes epitaphios of 1407, although strictly liturgical in its iconography, has as inscription a quotation from the troparion for Good Friday evening which clearly links it with the Crucifixion. The Cozia epitaphios of 1396 is one of the earliest of the existing examples to include the figures of the Virgin and St. John mourning the dead Saviour. From then on all epitaphioi, while they retained the classic decoration of the liturgical type, transformed this into the true Lamentation at the Tomb, the Orthodox equivalent of the Pietà, and the scene grew steadily more elaborate. The whole iconography is discussed in detail in Chapter IV.

The epitaphios can be regarded as the most important vehicle for embroidery in the Orthodox church and the one on which embroiderers expended their best efforts. The strictly regulated iconography did not leave the designer as much scope for invention as his counterpart in the west could enjoy in working on a cope or a frontal, but the large size of the veil (frequently nearly two metres long) allowed space for a monumental approach to the composition, which at its best reflected something of the awe-inspiring simplicity of Byzantine mosaics. The Salonica epitaphios stands as the supreme monument of Byzantine embroidery.

[27] In speaking of this veil the word sindon is usually omitted.

26

CHAPTER FOUR

ICONOGRAPHY

The idea that embroidery design should be an artistic expression particularly suited to the medium is a modern one, but even today, in spite of the careful distinction made between a panel and an embroidered picture, embroidery tends to follow closely trends set by artists in other fields. Embroiderers in the past saw nothing unusual in following or copying the work of painters, and even aspired to produce work which resembled a painting as closely as possible. Indeed the highest praise which writers of all periods have found for embroidery has been to describe it as painting with a needle.

Medieval church embroidery was nearly always narrative in subject rather than purely decorative, and followed very closely the style current in the greater arts, probably because of the versatility of the artist-craftsman who could work with equal ease in several media. It is unlikely that most embroidery designers specialised in this art alone. Decorative effects were frequently borrowed from architecture and the minor arts as well as from painting. Fourteenth century needleworkers, however, seem to have been content with the results produced by their own techniques, especially where colour was concerned, and did not attempt to copy the work of painters exactly, as was the case in later centuries. This was even more true of Byzantium than of the west, but even so the subjects chosen for Byzantine embroidery and the pictorial treatment of them were modelled very closely on the traditions established by mosaicists and fresco painters.

It must be emphasised that it was the monumental painters who influenced embroidery design, which seems to have had little in common with the art of the ivory carvers or the miniature painters, lacking the Hellenistic grace of the one and the surrealist elegance of the other, while it never matched either in freedom of invention and catholicity of subject. This is a little surprising in view of the fact that embroidery in Byzantine times was certainly a 'court' as opposed to a popular art, so that one might expect a more sophisticated taste.

The insistence on a rigid iconography was undoubtedly due to the close connection with the Liturgy which was observed both in the decoration of the church itself and in the vestments used in the church. At the same time the Byzantine technique of carrying out all the figure embroidery in gold thread favoured the monumental style and made the refinement and lively expression of miniature painting an impossibility.

The embroidered figure

Because of the very strong feeling always present in the Orthodox church that the Divine Liturgy is celebrated by the whole church in Heaven and earth together, the figures of the saints were so placed round the walls of the church that the communicant could feel they were actually present, ready to lead and guide him on the earthly road to paradise that they themselves had once trodden. Diez has described the church as one vast iconostasis covered with pictures of the saints, whose purpose, whether they were in mosaic on the walls or painted on icons, was to draw the beholder to their spiritual strength.[28] Figures of the saints were used in the same way to decorate vestments.

Presumably because of technical problems of space, the representation of single figures in embroidery belonged almost exclusively to the stole, whether priests's or deacon's, all other vestments being decorated with scenes drawn from the Gospels or apocryphal works or commentaries.

The head and shoulders of the Christ Pantocrator, the All-Powerful, with His hand eternally raised in blessing, is portrayed in terrible splendour in the domes of Byzantine churches. This is not the gentle figure of the Gospels, but the Godhead Incarnate, embodying in Himself both the awful majesty and the limitless compassion of Christianity. While the figure of Christ as He is shown in scenes from His earthly life is Jesus the Man, the Pantocrator is unmistakably God the Son, at one with the Creator of all things visible and invisible and with the all-pervading Power of the Holy Spirit.

In this light it is not difficult to understand why the Pantocrator is often placed in the centre of the stole which, it must be remembered, is the distinguishing insignia of the priesthood. Unfortunately, although the roundel on the back of a stole may represent liturgically the place of honour, it does not leave much space for dramatic portrayal with the needle, and the embroidered Pantocrator becomes a symbol rather than the overpowering Presence of the mosaics. There appears to be no case of a Pantocrator in embroidery worked on a scale which would allow characterisation.

There are occasional instances of the youthful Christ Emmanuel, representing

---

[28] E. Diez, O. Demus, Byzantine Mosaics in Greece, 1931, p. 33.

the Resurrection and the Life, embroidered on the neck of a stole.[29]

From the date of the Council of Ephesus which in 431 declared her Mother of God, the *Panagia*, the Most Holy, the Virgin is also treated in Byzantine iconography as an awe-inspiring and tragic figure. She is not the young mother gazing with tenderness and joy at her first born who was portrayed by so many western painters, but a woman who bears patiently on her shoulders all the sorrows of earthly motherhood and already feeels the shadow of the Cross falling on her Child. Even the Virgin of the Annunciation is not a joyous young girl on the eve of marriage, but stands in humble awe and sometimes even in fear before the Archangel, as if already conscious of the tragedy embodied in his message.

The Virgin on the stoles is frequently paired with St. John the Baptist. They stand on either side of the Christ in the traditional position of the Deisis, a favourite subject for icons which symbolised their intercession with the Almighty on behalf of the beholder of the icon. The figures on the stoles may be in roundels on the neck, in which case head and shoulders only are shown, or in the first arcades of the stole proper, when they are usually represented full length.   **31-32**

Alternatively the Virgin of the Annunciation is placed on one side of the stole and the angel on the other. In either case the Virgin is shown standing in an attitude of grave humility.

The Virgin figures in many Gospel scenes illustrated in embroidery, but it has already been mentioned in connection with the podea that an embroidered Virgin and Child is rare. It is perhaps also worth mentioning that the conception of the Coronation of the Virgin is entirely western. The story was told in the Golden Legend, which was written towards the end of the thirteenth century by an archbishop of Genoa, that is to say it caught the imagination of the west well after the Schism between the two churches. It therefore does not figure in Byzantine iconography at all, and the Virgin Crowned does not occur in Orthodox church embroidery until the late seventeenth and early eighteenth centuries, when certain designers deliberately turned to the west for fresh inspiration.

The Baptist is invariably given the traditional wild hair and flowing beard, but is usually dressed in the long tunic and overmantle thought appropriate to figures of Christ's lifetime. In mosaic and fresco he is often represented wearing a garment of skins, but embroiderers appear to have found this too difficult and did not attempt it. Western medieval embroiderers never attempted a realistic representation of fur either, but made full use of the heraldic device of *vair* to indicate fur in clothing.

The single figures of Apostles and Saints, the Early Fathers and the Prophets, who are portrayed in the arcaded sections of a stole are drawn with strict attention

[29] Millet, Broderies, pl. LVIII.

to iconographical ' correctness ', as were all figures in Byzantine art. Otto Demus has discussed at length the effect of the iconoclast controversy on figure representation.[30] When the ban on figures was eventually lifted, great stress was laid on the fact that the portrait was not holy in itself (i.e., an idol) but only aroused holy thoughts in the mind of the beholder by recalling the real object of veneration. For this reason figures were supposed to be shown frontally to achieve as realistic a relationship with the beholder as possible. This proved impracticable in every case, since figures taking part in a scene could have no relationship with each other if all looked to the front, and this difficulty in the end produced the three-quarter representation which is almost the hall-mark of Byzantine iconography.

There was of course no reason why isolated figures on a stole should not be shown frontally, and on many stoles this was done. On the other hand, by the fourteenth and fifteenth centuries the three-quarter view had become so much a part of the tradition that the figures are often made to face each other in pairs.

A further explanation of the iconographical difference between the formal frontal representation of saints and the more animated three-quarter view is offered by Turdeanu.[31] He accounts for the two distinct styles found in fifteenth century stoles by claiming that certain saints, particularly the Early Fathers and bishops, were represented in a traditional hieratic manner, their solemn frontal stance indicating meekness, submission to the will of God, and a mood of contemplation. The Prophets and Apostles, however, were seen as figures filled with missionary zeal and accordingly shown in lively movement. The artist, he says, attributes to them ' l'énergie des inspirés par le Verbe et répresente certains d'entre eux en pleine agitation de leur vocation '. It was possible to combine the two styles in a single stole according to the character represented.

For the same reason, great attention was paid to the ' correct ' representation, according to early tradition, of the physical attributes and dress of a particular person. This kind of characterisation was carried out in embroidery as in any other medium.

Figures were placed in rigid categories as far as their clothes were concerned but in fact the dress used for each group was reasonably accurate. A difference was made between Old and New Testament characters, the latter wearing chiton and himation without ornament. The Early Fathers of the Church were dressed as bishops in sticharion with potamoi and cuff ornament, phelonion, epitrachilion, omophorion, and sometimes epigonation, the last usually shown in the form of a towel rather than the later stiffened square.

[30] O. Demus, Byzantine Mosaic Decoration, 1948, p. 7.
[31] Turdeanu, Les étoles, pp. 35-6, 59.

30

Embroiderers seldom showed the phelonion decorated with crosses, and the exceptions are all Serbian work. Whether this was because they were aware that it would have been an anachronism, or because they baulked the technical difficulties involved in a small space it is impossible to say. Probably the second explanation is the right one, since when space allowed, for example in the Chilandari curtain, both St. John Chrysostom and St. Basil are shown in the *polystavrion*, which was not in fact in use until several centuries after their day. Portraits of donors, which were a speciality of the Rumanian embroideries, were also correctly dressed in the costume of their time and provide an important historical record.

40-42

The parallel drawn in the church between deacons and angels has already been mentioned. Angels therefore could be treated either as part of the heavenly hierarchy or as the servitors of heaven. In the first case they were dressed in the chiton and himation which were thought appropriate to Christ's lifetime. The Angel of the Annunciation naturally always appears in this form. On the other hand the heavenly servants, whose particular role was to guard the Body of Christ, whether it was presented in its actual or its liturgical form, were dressed as deacons of the church, that is to say in sticharion and orarion. They also carried fans, with which it had once been the duty of the deacon, particularly in the Syrian church, to keep the flies from the Sacred Elements, but which later became a symbol of office. When space allowed the orarion was correctly decorated with cherubim and the thrice-repeated ἅγιος. With the same analogy in mind, angels were sometimes also dressed in imperial costume, that is as servants of the King of Heaven.

Both angel types are illustrated in embroidery and often occur together on the epitaphioi, but it must be admitted that few, if any, embroiderers achieved the refined, almost sexless beauty of the ringleted Greek god which represented to the Byzantine the angelic ideal, and which was brought to perfection in the hands of the icon painters. Embroidery designers were at their best in handling the mourning angels of the epitaphioi, whose wings and draperies are treated with a grace of movement which conveys a real emotion.

96, 102

Byzantine insistence on the portrayal of the soul in the human face at the expense of individuality in the body, allied to the eastern style of linear drawing, gradually devised a system which gave the maximum spirituality to faces, partly by the emphasis on and enlargement of the eyes in relation to the other features, but largely by the careful arrangement of lines on the forehead and round the eyes which produced a classic range of entirely imaginary portraits with the compelling spiritual power of genuine likenesses. A careful and formal arrangement of lines was used for hair, which resulted in a typical pattern of curls or waves for each individual. Any representation of St. Peter shows this clearly. Christ and the angels and many others have their own hair patterns, and these were followed closely by embroiderers as well as mosaicists.

58, 96, 103

By the same token the natural moulding of the body was clothed in draperies presented as a stylised arrangement of lines, which eventually became a formal pattern in their own right. The linear composition of features, hair and draperies can be studied at its best in mosaics and icons, but will be seen to have a particular importance for embroidery techniques.

Narrative Scenes

The artistic renaissance of the tenth and eleventh centuries which followed the settlement of the iconoclast troubles brought with it a change in the attitude of the church towards pictorial art. During earlier centuries illustrations of the Bible stories had been regarded not merely as a means of adorning a building to make it a fit place for the worship of God, but above all as a way of teaching the faithful and presenting the scriptures to the illiterate. Scenes from both Old and New Testaments were chosen, and the whole of Christ's earthly life was presented in detail, roughly in the order described in the Gospels.

By the eleventh century the emphasis had shifted from doctrine to dogma. Christianity was by this time so firmly established that the teaching of the factual happenings of scripture was taken for granted. Instead stress was laid on the meaning of the deeper mysteries of the faith, the road through share in Christ's sacrifice to the ultimate salvation and the part played by each Christian soul, whether in this world or the next, in the great Christian community of the saints and angels. To this end certain scenes from the life of Christ came to be regarded as expressing the essentials of Christian dogma and were given particular prominence in specific positions in the decoration of a church. These twelve scenes, covering the Great Feasts of the Church, occur with occasional variations from this time onwards not only in the decoration of churches but in all other artistic media. They are frequently encountered in embroidery, either together or individually. They are:

> Annunciation
> Nativity
> Presentation in the Temple
> Baptism
> Raising of Lazarus
> Transfiguration
> Entry into Jerusalem
> Crucifixion
> Descent into Hell or Resurrection
> Ascension
> Pentecost
> Dormition of the Virgin

The Resurrection (the Anastasis) was usually represented in the eastern church from 51 the time of the Macedonian dynasty (tenth/eleventh centuries) by the scene that was known in the west as the Harrowing of Hell. This is the story from the apocryphal gospel of Nicodemus of Christ's descent into Hell, where He is shown holding the Cross on high and breaking the gates of Hell (or sometimes the body of Satan) under His feet, while He stretches out a hand to lead Adam and Eve from the pit. John the Baptist is present, since the story of his preaching in Hell is stressed in Nicodemus, and the prophets who bore witness to the redemption of mankind through the Resurrection are usually represented by the Prophet Kings, David and Solomon. Earlier the scene of the Two Maries at the Sepulchre had been used to illustrate the Resurrection, but the Anastasis is more usual in embroidery, which is all late enough in date for its use to have become traditional.

The Dormition, or falling asleep, of the Virgin is the eastern equivalent of the 57 Assumption. The Mother of God is shown lying on a bier surrounded by the mourning figures of the Apostles. Above the bier Christ receives the soul of His Mother in the form of a child. In the foreground St. Michael slashes the hands from the upraised arms of Jephonias, who, according to the apocryphal story, had presumed to touch the bier.

Byzantine art of the eleventh and twelfth centuries retained some of the austerity of earlier years tempered by the elegant style of the linear compositions. Iconography was reduced to essentials so that a direct and uncluttered picture emphasised the dogmatic principle. Nevertheless at about this time an increasing feeling of tenderness and compassion began to replace the austere mood and continued to grow steadily through the next three centuries. Side by side with this sympathy for the human emotions, a movement developed which continually enriched and enlarged the details of the iconography. Artists sought a closer acquaintance with the scenes they were illustrating from the apocryphal gospels, and from commentators on the Gospels from St. John Chrysostom to the twelfth century writer Metarites.

It must be emphasised that no detail of Byzantine iconography in any medium was included according to the whim or imagination of the artist. A designer who wished to depart in the smallest particular from tradition could only search the Gospels or the accepted interpreters for further information on his theme, and every apparently haphazard circumstance, whether the Virgin of the Annunciation sits or stands, the exact position of her hand and so on, is firmly based on hallowed writings.

During the same period western artists were also studying the apocryphal gospels for details of the Bible stories, but the two churches tended to rely on different writers. Western artists working on the Annunciation relied on Pseudo-Matthew, who emphasised the young girl's piety and learning, but left out the story of the meeting with the angel at the well and Mary's return to her spinning afterwards. Italian painters therefore showed the Virgin reading or praying when the angel came to her. In the same way the introduction of a lily was a detail first used in the west and later copied in the Orthodox church.

69

The scenes of the Great Feasts, sometimes with fourteenth century additions, such as the Flagellation, the Doubting of Thomas, the Road to Damascus, which were part of the later elaboration of iconography, are found in embroidery on the more elaborate stoles. Occasionally they occur round the central scene on curtains for the iconostasis, and in one isolated instance eight of the Feasts are represented on a pair of epimanikia.

29, 35, 36

59, 66

Fitting one of these scenes into a compartment of a stole meant cramming a great deal of detail into a very small space (about four or five inches square). Since gold thread embroidery is not the best medium for this exercise, most designers abandoned the niceties of fourteenth century iconography and the formation of a composite picture by the addition of related events (for example, the journey of the Magi as part of the Nativity) and reduced each scene to its essentials. This simplification was certainly due to technical difficulties and in no way intended as a return to the bold statement of dogma of Macedonian times. When an embroiderer felt he had room or was technically competent enough, random items of the later iconography appear to have been added according to taste. Two very sophisticated stoles with the Great Feasts, probably of the sixteenth century and certainly from highly expert workrooms, exist in the monasteries of the Great Lavra and Iviron on Mount Athos.[32] Their workers have managed to include almost every detail required by Gospel and Apocrypha.

Embroiderers were on the whole much less adventurous in their choice of subject than the fresco painters who worked at the same period and who were abandoning the strict liturgical cycle in favour of more elaborate schemes. The scenes chosen to decorate vestments were relatively few and the majority of them belonged to the Twelve Feasts. Even so, only a few of these were used regularly outside the cycle itself. The favourites were the Annunciation on epitrachilia and epimanikia, and the Transfiguration and Anastasis on epigonatia. Ascension, Pentecost and Dormition are found occasionally, the Nativity, Baptism, Raising of Lazarus and Entry into Jersualem very seldom. Greater freedom is often found in the iconography of podeai and sanctuary curtains than in that of the priestly vestments. The curtain sent by Michael VIII Palaeologus to Pope Gregory X at the time of the Council of Lyons in 1274, which has not survived but which seems to have been designed in a style which was copied later (see p. 77), suggests that the Acts of the Apostles provided traditional subjects for hangings.

[32] Millet, Broderies, pls. CX-CXII, CXVI-VII.

34

Outside the Feasts, the Communion of the Apostles was used regularly to 85-90 decorate the Little Aër. Emphasis on the mystical nature of the sacrament chose this scene in preference to the more literal illustration of the Bible story of the Last Supper. In it Christ is shown standing at an altar, which is distinguished from an ordinary table by the addition of a ciborium. He offers the Bread or Chalice to His followers, who line up on each side to receive the sacrament. The altar is often attended by angel/deacons with fans.

An increasing leaning towards mysticism eventually replaced this traditional 91 scene on the Little Aër with the Christ Child laid in the patten to represent the Lamb of God, the emblem of sacrifice. This conception clearly reverts to the very early use of the Lamb on the aër before it was forbidden in the seventh century. The idea, which Gabriel Millet has described as ' charmante et cruelle ',[33] appears to have found special favour in Serbia and Rumania, where it occurs in the fresco painting. It was used in some of the Serb churches as early as the fourteenth century, and is found on the outside of the apse of the monastery church of Vatra-Moldoviței, which was painted during the sixteenth. Likewise a Serbian aër at Chilandari, probably dating from the fourteenth century, is embroidered with this subject, but in Rumania and elsewhere it is not found before the end of the sixteenth century.

Byzantine mysticism also conceived the idea of using Abraham's hospitality to the three angels at Mamre (Genesis 18, 1-8) as an illustration of the Trinity. The famous rendering of this scene on an early fifteenth century icon by the Russian painter Andrei Rublev merely shows the three angels seated at table under the tree mentioned in the biblical text. This treatment is repeated in embroidery on the crown of a mitre from Esphigmenou, but a very fine podea from the Rumanian Athonite monastery of Grigoriou,[34] which may have come from the Moldavian workrooms of Stephen the Great, elaborates the iconography. Abraham and Sarah have joined the angels round the table, and in the front of the picture, as a secondary scene complementary to the main action, Abraham is shown cutting the throat of the sacrificial calf.

Reverence for the Mother of God had caused iconographers to search apocryphal sources as well as the Gospels for details of her life, and to build up a traditional cycle of illustration on the subject as early as the eleventh century, which included apocryphal details such as the distaff at the Annunciation and the presence of the midwife Salome at the Nativity, as well as the story of Jephonias already mentioned. The hymn called the Acathistos dealt in twenty-four strophes with the Life of the Virgin and the Childhood of Christ. Illustration of the verses

[33] Millet, Broderies, p. 74.
[34] Op. cit., pls. CLXX-I.

of the Acathistos became increasingly popular with the fresco painters from the fourteenth century on, again particularly in the monasteries of Mount Athos. The Holy Mountain also preserves one of the few pieces of embroidery to deal with the subject, a stole at Stavronikita.[35] (There is another much later stole in the Treasury of the Oecumenical Patriarchate at Istanbul.) Commenting on this piece, Millet has pointed out that the coming of Christ was a theme often called to mind on a stole by the use of the Prophets and the Annunciation, and that the Acathistos was therefore particularly suited to this vestment. To fit the whole twenty-four strophes into the length of a stole with any clarity was no mean technical feat, and the Stavronikita epitrachilion was obviously produced by highly skilled workers.

The Lamentation

Since the epitaphios holds such an important place among the embroidered vestments, it is worth examining rather more fully the iconography both of the earlier, liturgical type and of the Lamentation as it is represented on the true epitaphios. Ştefanescu has discussed at some length the decoration of the Great Aër or the processional veil which is called epitaphios, in which the emphasis was less on mourning for the dead Christ than on liturgical significance and heavenly glorification,[36] and it will be seen that every single item is directly connected with the words and meaning of the Liturgy. The main feature of the veil was the Body of Christ, representing the mystical transformation of the Bread and Wine, which lay on the Red Stone of Ephesus. This was the stone which traditionally had been used for the embalming after the Crucifixion. It had been preserved afterwards at Ephesus, and was brought by the Byzantines during the twelfth century to Constantinople, where it was kept in the church of the Pantocrator. It is said that the Emperor Manuel Comnenus carried it there on his back from the city gates. The bier shown in most liturgical epitaphioi represents this stone. The Body is nimbed with a cross halo and clothed only in a loin cloth. The Wounds in the side and on hands and feet are clearly shown.

Traditionally the decoration of the sanctuary illustrated the related themes of Judgment and Salvation, with special emphasis laid on the remission of sins through the Eucharist. The concept of Judgment was iconographically represented by the Son of Man, or sometimes by the Prepared Throne (Psalm 9, 7. ' He hath prepared his throne for the judgement '), surrounded and glorified by the Beasts of the Apocalypse and the heavenly powers (Revelation, 4, 6-9). The epitaphios, symbol of the Eucharist, embraced the associated themes of Judgment and praise by the inclusion of the Four Beasts in the corners of the veil. Like the four-headed

[35] Millet, Broderies, pp. 56-7, pls. CXIII-CXV.
[36] Ştefanescu, Voiles, p. 103ff.

cherubim of Ezekiel's vision (Ezekiel 1, 5-11), the Beasts of the Apocalypse were linked by the theologians with the Four Gospels, and thus yet another meaning could be given to their presence: they represented the way to Salvation through the expressed word of God in His Gospel.

For a long period the Orthodox church did not admit the Book of Revelation to the canon, and even after its recognition iconographers tended to cover their interpretations by linking the Beasts of the Apocalypse to Ezekiel's tetramorphs. Hence their tendency to show the head and shoulders only of the Beasts, hiding the bodies behind an arc of glory, and so indicating four heads with a single body. Even on the epitaphioi, where the four are separated, a section of the arc remains.[37]   102
In some examples this was used to contribute to the theme of glorification, announcing the hymn of praise in the mouths of the Beasts, 'Holy, holy, holy' (Revelation 4, 8) by embroidering in the four arcs the words which introduce the Sanctus in the Liturgy: ᾄδοντα, βοῶντα, κεκραγότα, λέγοντα ('*Singing, crying, shouting* and *saying* the triumphal hymn: Holy, holy, holy, Lord God of Sabaoth '.)[38]
In a very few epitaphioi the Evangelists are represented not by their symbols but by the men themselves.

99

The veil is especially connected with the liturgical procession called the Great Entry, which was compared as early as the eighth century[39] by Germanus of Constantinople to the Entry into Jerusalem: 'The carrying of the Elements, I mean of the Body and Blood of the Lord, from the prothesis and their entry to the altar and the cherubic hymn signify the entry of the Lord into Jerusalem from Bethany. For then a great multitude and the children of the Hebrews clearly addressed their hymn as it were to the king and the victor over death, and spiritually the angels with the cherubim sang as their hymn the trisagion: and the sceptres and the fans the deacons bear as royal insignia '.[40]   The Body is therefore surrounded by the angels and the cherubim and the wheels of Ezekiel (1, 15-18),   96
glorifying God, and by the sun, moon and stars, which take their part in the   106
outpouring of praise (Psalm 148, 3. 'Praise ye him, sun and moon, praise him all ye stars of light.').   In addition, since the Body is also the Eucharist, it is guarded by deacon/angels bearing fans with the word ἅγιος, the first word both of the Sanctus and that part of the Liturgy called the Trisagion (' Holy God, Holy and Strong, Holy and Immortal, Have mercy upon us ').

[37] Millet, La Dalmatique, p. 50.

[38] The onomatopoeic words are intended to represent the sounds made by the Beasts symbolising the Evangelists.

[39] It does not follow that the decorated processional veil was used as early as this. It seems more likely that this custom orginated in the fourteenth century.

[40] Ștefanescu, Voiles, p. 105.

The simplest liturgical iconography, of which the lost epitaphios of St.
93 Clement was a good example, admitted no emotion, either of glorification or of
99 mourning. It is repeated over the following century, the Nicholas Eudaimonoioannes epitaphios being one of the latest. A slightly different treatment of the
94 theme is found in the epitaphios of Milutin Ureš, which is of about the same
date as St. Clement and was also repeated over the next hundred years or more.
This lays all the emphasis on the glorification of the Christ by angels and heavenly
powers. Bier, deacons and Evangelists are omitted. Milutin Ureš itself is unusual
in that the Christ is treated with greater formality and appears almost to be
standing rather than lying, while a little aër is shown covering the Body in place
of a loin cloth. It is the only example where the aër is worked into the design.[41]
There are two seraphim and six angels praising God with the words Holy, holy,
holy. Other designers added the winged wheels studded with eyes to the worship-
ping Powers.

It was customary in the church to hold objects of great veneration, such as
the Communion vessels and the Gospels, not with the naked hand but covered
in a cloth. The Apostles approaching Christ to receive the Bread and Wine and
the Evangelists holding their sacred writings are often shown for this reason with
their sleeves covering their hands. It is evidently in this tradition that the angels
94 on Milutin Ureš hold out their hands covered with their garments as if they
prepared to receive the holy Body.

Their attitude here is one of worship, but the first step in the direction of the
sorrow of the Lamentation is the introduction of mourning angels into the rather
93, 96 severe composition typified by St. Clement. The famous Salonica epitaphios,
the greatest of those surviving from the fourteenth century, has the basic elements
of St. Clement, but the theme of worship is also represented by seraphim and
cherubim. In addition to the two deacon/angels there is another who leans towards
the Body with covered hands, and a fourth who hides his face in horror. Most of
the later epitaphioi have at least one, if not several, angels weeping or gesticulating
as well as the deacons. Seraphim and cherubim tend to be dropped as the iconography becomes more elaborate and space is lacking.

As we have seen, the representation of the Crucified Christ on the Great
Aër was intended as a concrete expression of the mystical change in the consecrated
Bread and Wine. The Christ of the epitaphios sindon, although outwardly the
Man crucified and mourned by His Mother and friends, was also intended to
recall the deeper theological meaning to the minds of the congregation who
watched the veil carried in procession, but it was towards the end of the fourteenth

---

[41] The aër in the corner of St. Clement which can be seen in the photographs was not part of the
original, but was an actual aër added later as a repair.

century, when the role of the epitaphios in the Liturgy changed again, that the theme of mourning came into its own.

One of the earliest surviving examples to include the figures of the Lamentation is the one from Cozia, now at Bucharest. This is a very simple version. The Mother of God bends forward from behind the bier to embrace her dead Son, and St. John stands at the foot of the stone. There are four deacons but no heavenly powers and no Evangelists.

The iconography of the Lamentation is based on the apocryphal gospel of Nicodemus. Two distinct styles were developed from later interpreters.[42] The first of these follows George of Nicomedia. The Mother of God is described as flinging herself on the divine body to bathe it with scalding tears, and she leans forward, as in Cozia, to kiss the lips and eyes of the Saviour. This version occurs in fresco and icon painting (for example in the twelfth century frescoes of St. Panteleimon at Nerezi[43]), and was painted in the west by both Duccio and Giotto. It is the version used in the earliest epitaphioi (Cozia and Syropoulos) and it is noticeable that they are of Byzantine or Serbo-Byzantine origin.[44]

In the second version, after the meditations of St. Bonaventura, Mary took the head and shoulders of the Saviour in her lap when He was lifted from the Cross. This first occurs in embroidery in the Moldavian epitaphios of Neamţ (1437), and one must ask whether it is an instance of western influence. The known epitaphioi for the rest of the fifteenth century are all Moldavian and follow Neamţ in this respect.[45] By the sixteenth century this version had superseded the other in all epitaphioi.

In the earlier iconography reverence would permit none but the Mother to touch the sacred Body. Later a growing realism and a more emotional interpretation of the scene allowed St. John to hold His hand and to bend to kiss it. Gradually all the friends of Jesus whom the Gospels record as present at His Crucifixion

[42] Millet, Recherches sur l'iconographie de l'Evangile, Paris, 1916, p. 489.
[43] Cecil Stewart, Serbian Legacy, 1959, p. 44.
[44] A small Greek epitaphios in the Ikonenmuseum Schloss Autenried also has this version of the scene. A date of 1400 has been suggested for this piece on the strength of the letters *Alpha Ypsilon* in the inscription (B. Rothemund, Byzantinische u. russische kirchliche Stickereien, Slavisches Institut München, 1961, p. 16). These letters do give 1400, but Byzantine dates at this period were reckoned from the Creation, and 1400 A.D. would have been expressed as 6908 (see notes on dating Chap. VI, p. 51 below). The piece has been very much restored and transferred to a velvet background, while that part of the border inscription which appears to contain the dedication is so worn as to be practically illegible, and one side is apparently missing altogether. The fact that the Virgin is shown embracing Christ from behind the bier would be compatible with an early date, but other features, such as a ciborium over the scene and the style of the inscription, suggest that it should be dated much later. At least one Greek designer of the eighteenth century reintroduced this early version of the position of the Virgin.
[45] Some examples exist in Russia from the middle of the fifteenth century, and these follow this version.

are introduced into the composition, starting with St. Joseph of Arimathea, who holds His feet, and Mary Magdalene, the most dramatic and passionately emotional figure in the group.

After St. Joseph and Mary Magdalene, Nicodemus was added, and the other Maries, the wife of Cleophas and the mother of James and Joses, and later Salome and Joanna. These women are sometimes, particularly in very late examples, labelled by name, but they are more often represented by a group of two or three and simply called 'the spice-bearing women' ($\mu\upsilon\rho o\phi\acute{o}\rho o\iota$). In point of fact the embroideries only developed the iconography at a very late date. The whole story, as elaborated by the commentators, had been told in all its details in painting and fresco, both in east and west, by the earliest years of the fourteenth century.

The Syropoulos epitaphios at Chilandari (see p. 80 below) is much the earliest embroidery to foreshadow further elaboration of the scene in the sixteenth century, which added the Cross behind the bier, with the instruments of the Passion, the vessels holding the spices for the embalming, the ladder and other details. By the end of this century the Cross with its appurtenances and all the mourners had become usual, as well as Evangelists, deacons and angels. The Body was often laid, not on the bier itself, but on the linen cloth provided by St. Joseph. By the end of the seventeenth and the eighteenth century we find some of the more sophisticated workrooms crowding the design with even more detail, in the shape of architectural scenes representing the City of Jerusalem, Golgotha and the Mount of Olives. At the same time a so-called peasant style developed, which kept the main features but tended to simplification and a much cruder presentation.

On the other hand, one of the greatest designers of this late period, Despoineta of Constantinople, turned deliberately from the over-loaded iconography, and not only simplified the scene but, by placing a ciborium over the stone to recall its function as an altar, re-emphasised the ancient conception of the Body as the visible emblem of the mystical change in the Bread and Wine.

CHAPTER FIVE

ORNAMENT

When the iconoclast controversy was finally resolved, the Church's demand for an unequivocal doctrinal statement in art made it essential that figures and scenes should be presented without unnecessary distractions. A clear distinction was made between subject and ornament, and the latter was relegated to a framework, a dividing band, an unfilled surface.

This rule was applied throughout the arts to the purely decorative element in a composition, but at the same time mosaicists and painters developed an almost mathematical approach to questions of line and balance, and eventually produced a system of linear figure drawing which embodied in itself a whole theory of ornament. This somewhat mannered form of expression was, of course, carried over into the minor arts, embroidery among them, but although the embroideries were considerably influenced by the style and developed their own methods of dealing with it, the techniques employed were too rigid to realise its full ornamental effect. In fact the more fluid embroidery methods of the fourteenth century in western Europe were capable of handling the Byzantine linear style with greater ease and elegance.

However, if Byzantine gold embroiderers could not fully imitate painters and mosaicists in the decorative grace of their figure drawing, their technique produced its own form of subsidiary ornament. It is a feature of gold thread embroidery that the stitches must necessarily produce a pattern of some kind, even if it is only a simple, alternating brick device. The changes that could be rung on these patterns provided a whole scheme of decoration within the figure subject itself, in the same way that the linear extravaganzas of other artists treated the human figure as an ornamental composition. All this is quite separate from and subordinate to the true ornament of the background and surrounding borders, which is our concern in this chapter. (Stitchery patterns will be discussed under Technique, Chapter VIII.)

The earliest embroideries on the whole relied less on elaborate decorative effect. The distinguishing mark of the thirteenth and fourteenth centuries was

107

above all the cross in a circle. This was used singly as a background motif, either
scattered as in the Vatican saccos and the epigonation in the Byzantine Museum
in Athens, or in more formal rows (the epitaphioi of St. Clement and St. Mark.)
The single device was quickly transformed into a border of linked circles (the
Salonica epitaphios) and into every combination that could be devised of the
cross-and-circle and square-and-circle, whether as border or interlocking background patterns. Many early embroideries had narrow, unobtrusive borders,
consisting very often of a simple, formal scrolling stem and leaf design (the Genoa
altar cloth, the John of Skopje epitaphios). The scrolling stem terminating in a
leaf is also used as a background pattern, although this is much rarer. It is found
on the bottom border of the Vatican saccos, on the Grandson frontal (which has
circular flower shapes instead of leaves) and, at a later date, on the Nicholas
Eudaimonoioannes epitaphios.

As far as can be seen from the limited material available from this period, the
plainer style, and particularly the single scattered cross-in-a-circle and the simple
scrolling border, was originally Greek, probably Constantinopolitan. More
elaborate variations seem to have become popular, especially for stoles, towards
the end of the fourteenth century. These twining and interlocking patterns,
whose lines crossed and recrossed in a never-ending maze, are strongly Arabic in
flavour. The abstract decoration of Islamic art, which spread widely throughout
the Near East in the days of Baghdad's splendour in the ninth century, gained
ground in Christian art in this period through its particular appeal for the iconoclasts. Dalton has drawn attention to the common roots shared by Early Christian
and Islamic art,[46] and goes so far as to suggest that East Christian art in later
centuries might hardly have differed from the art of Islam if the iconoclasts had
been eventually victorious.

This type of ornament seems to fall into two categories, the first composed
of sinuous lines twisting in elaborate scrolls and loops, very frequently embodying
heart shapes and sometimes animal forms and stylised flowers. The patterns were
thickly concentrated and covered the ground space closely. The style is found at
its most typical in Greek stoles from the late fourteenth and first half of the fifteenth centuries, or in stoles which may have been copied from Greek models.

Both animals and hearts are of Islamic origin. Heart shapes were popular
in the roundel borders in Byzantine silks. The animal motifs of the embroideries,
on the other hand, have nothing in common with the magnificent lions and eleph-
ants of the silks. They are also much less exotic than the weird apparitions bred
in Mesopotamia and Scythia, and are in general confined to very few types. These
include lion-masks, dragons of an inoffensive and somewhat domesticated type,

[46] O. M. Dalton. East Christian Art, 1925, p. 16.

42

long, snake-like dragon heads, actual snakes and birds.[47] They largely died out with the change in ornamental style at the end of the fifteenth century, but birds especially remained popular where this tortuous decoration persisted. Combined with the twined heart motif they became in the end very close to some peasant embroideries in the Balkans. The imperial double-headed eagle sometimes occurs in late Byzantine and post-Byzantine embroideries and is said to indicate that the vestment had some connection with the Patriarchate in Constantinople.[48]

33

The second kind of interlace ornament seems in some cases very closely connected with the first and almost to develop from it, but it is much more geometric, more closely related to the purely abstract Arabic style, and based almost entirely on square-and-circle combinations. This type of decoration, which was evident in all-over background patterns as well as in ornamental bands and end panels on stoles, started to replace the more elaborate style in the second half of the fifteenth century, and seems to have been particularly popular in Serbia and Macedonia and later in Rumania.

38

The cross-in-a-circle, besides providing the basis of many interlocking designs, developed in the Serbian epitaphioi of the fourteenth century into powdered background patterns of cross/stars and star/flowers (the Milutin Ureš and Euphemia and Eupraxia epitaphioi). The stars appeared as part of the hymn of praise, and were joined in later epitaphioi by the sun and moon. The interchange of star and flower motifs is found as early as the fifth century in vault decoration at Ravenna.

94, 97

Parallel to the border patterns of crosses and linked circles in the fourteenth century, the St. Clement epitaphios, from the last years of the preceding century, provided a classical border which was to be widely repeated in Serbia and Moldavia for the next three hundred years. This consisted basically of crosses in circles alternating with and linked to foliate devices composed of formal arabesque-like leaf shapes. The Syropoulos epitaphios at Chilandari is unique (in this as in other details) in that the border is composed of the disconnected foliate patterns without the linking circles and crosses.

The basic decorative scheme of the early stoles also appears to have been based on the linked circle. Figures of saints or scenes were contained in large circles, which were joined together by small ones in a never-ending chain, while the remaining space, and usually a band at the bottom as well, was filled with complicated pattern. This style seems to have continued in Greece, although in a

29

---

[47] A notable exception is the stole at the Lavra Monastery on Mount Athos, illustrated in Millet, Broderies, Pl. CXII, which has the heads of bulls, wolves, bears and lions in the bottom panels.

[48] Millet, Broderies, p. 36.

plainer form, after it had been discarded in the Balkans, and is linked with the older type of twining ornament.

During the fifteenth century, however, a strong tendency to simplify ornament on stoles developed. A Greek stole at Patmos, probably from the first half of the century, has lost the circles, which have been replaced by horizontal bands of ornament, dividing the length into separate compartments. The ornament, it should be noted, is in this case still very much in the old style, with scrolled stems and dragon heads. Rectangular compartments containing a circle were used in Moldavia in the stole of Stephen the Great and Alexander, and in other stoles at Putna, and the circle soon disappeared altogether, leaving a plain rectangle.

During the fifteenth century the first arcaded stoles appear. Architectural arcading used as an ornamental framework to set off and divide figure subjects had been a common device of relief sculpture and all the minor arts, both eastern and western, over a very long period. It had been used by western embroidery designers since the fourteenth century, but only seems to have been taken up in Orthodox embroidery nearly a hundred years later. The first piece to make use of the device appears to be the Great Saccos of the Metropolitan Photius from the second decade of the fifteenth century. As in all ornament of this type, the arches tended to reflect the actual architecture of the country and period concerned. In Greek stoles both the rounded Byzantine arch and the trilobed Islamic arch were used, and both were transmitted to the Balkans and Rumania. This type of ornament was to establish itself as the classic design for epitrachilia which lasted well into the nineteenth century. In the early examples the arcading was severe and unobtrusive and not heavily decorated. Lion masks were often used as capitals, a practice which occurs in manuscript illumination but does not otherwise appear to be a feature of Byzantine ornament, which in general treated lions in a more realistic and imposing way. The only parallel in embroidery appears to be with England in the fourteenth century, where the same mask was sometimes used in opus anglicanum (for example the Butler-Bowden cope). Occasionally in the Rumanian stoles leaf ornament sprouted from the base of the arch. The best known examples of this device were also from English embroidery of the late fourteenth century, but were carried to much greater lengths. In Rumania the leaf was small and stilted and never developed into the luxuriant foliage which which was typical of the English embroideries.

Arcaded stoles also had narrow bands of ornament dividing the sections. These bands were sometimes starkly composed of simple circle and square motifs, sometimes much more elaborate, frequently based on plaited or interlace elements, and all highly Islamic in character. Very many of them are paralleled in ornament in illuminated manuscripts.[49] At the same time ornament on the bottom of stoles and on epimanikia also became more geometric. Like the ground ornament

[49] M. Alison Frantz, Byzantine Illuminated Ornament, in THE ART BULLETIN, XVI, 1934, p. 43.

in the earlier Serbian embroideries, it was based mainly on permutations of circles and squares, but after the turn of the century and through the first half of the sixteenth century it became cruder and less elegant in effect. The swastika was a motif much in evidence in this type of pattern.

At this period the classic scrolling stem of the earlier embroideries took on a severe flattened form which is very typical of the late fifteenth and early sixteenth centuries. This was a fairly widely spread form of the *rinceau* which was found 19-21, 35 in Coptic sculpture but probably reached Rumanian embroidery by way of Islam. The elongated, pointed leaf shape, which is turned closely back against the flattened curve of the stem, is sometimes described as half a palmette.

The first half of the sixteenth century was a period when extravagant ornament was out of fashion. Stoles were divided by severe arcading, relieved sometimes by spiral columns (a common device in western embroidery of the period) but with little or no decoration in the spandrels. Others consisted simply of rectangles containing figures or scenes, which were sometimes divided by horizontal bands but quite often without even this relief. What ornament there was turned to a 43 bold stylisation which was the antithesis of the small intricate designs of the earlier 48, 61 periods. Other vestments such as epimanikia and podeai also relied more and more on artistic representation and less on extraneous ornamental backgrounds and borders. This meant that any decorative effect must be obtained from the gold embroidery within the figure subject itself, and it is noticeable that the sixteenth century was a time when stitchery patterns were at their most varied.

Although ornament in the embroideries went through several marked changes in the course of centuries, the workers were highly traditionalist, and these changes took place very slowly. The styles that have so far been discussed all arose from the Byzantine period proper, that is from the earliest known embroideries to the middle of the fifteenth century, and were repeated, if in a rather attentuated form, well into the sixteenth century. We have seen that the geometric interlocking patterns became simpler until they disappeared altogether. In the same way, the old twining ornament, which was still used on some stoles (probably Greek) in the sixteenth century, grew thin and lost its grace and richness. The originally Byzantine border of linked crosses and foliate patterns was still used in Rumania in the Movila embroideries at Suceviţa in the first years of the seventeenth century, 81, 82 but it was round about that time that the great change in decorative style took place.

From the last years of the sixteenth century, and increasingly during the next two hunded years, ornament again came back into fashion, so much so that by the eighteenth century almost as much attention was paid to the decorative borders 46 as to the scenes they surrounded. This tendency was certainly a general reflection of the feeling of the period, but must have been at least in part a protest against the hackneyed repetition of an outworn iconography.

The ornament that replaced the austerities of the mid-sixteenth century was not in the abstract Islamic style which had preceded them, but it still maintained the tradition laid down by Byzantium that textile decoration should derive from the east. The first group of embroideries to herald the new age were those made **68-70** for the church of the Three Hierarchs at Jassy in the time of Basil Lupu at the end of the 1630's, which in fact represented a last renaissance of the embroidery tradition in Moldavia. The leaf and flower ornament of their borders is clearly drawn from Persian carpets, and marks the beginning of a long period of increasing feeling for naturalistic floral decoration based on sixteenth century Persian flower motifs.

The elegant and highly characteristic flower painting of artists at the Safavid court, springing from a botanist's appreciation of the natural beauty of the garden flowers which were their models and transformed with sublety into a formal composition of line and balance, had its lasting effect on the minor arts of the Near East. The floral designs of Persian silks and carpets from the time of Shah Abbas I can be traced in the silks and pottery of Asia Minor in the following centuries, and had a very marked influence on embroidery decoration in Greece and the Balkans, both in professional ecclesiastical work and in folk art. In the group from the Three Hierarchs we not only find repeating border patterns, but single scattered flowers used as background motifs which have both the accurate **68** naturalism and the idealised grace of Persian drawing. The podea of the **69** Annunciation has a vase of flowers borrowed from the traditional western iconography of the lily, but here transformed into a purely Near Eastern motif. It is perhaps worth noting that at this period Moldavia had close connections with Poland, where Persian carpets and Persian silks for use as sashes were very popular.

At the same period a number of vestments, particularly in Wallachia, were made from imported Italian silks, and a few embroideries show Italianate detail in leaf and flower patterns. (The Italian silk industry was, of course, also greatly influenced by Near Eastern decoration.)

The seventeenth and early eighteenth centuries saw a revival of the arabesque background pattern in a highly ornamental form. The embryo leaves of the classic pattern are enlarged to a luxuriant foliage, the scrolling is elaborate and prolific, and every kind of flower blossoms in the encircling stems. This kind of ornament ranges from scrolling carnations firmly rooted in Asia Minor (the Alexandra Dena epimanikion in the Victoria and Albert Museum),[50] to a less naturalistic, purely decorative European rococo style.

The Constantinopolitan embroideress Despoineta, whose work did much to restore the fallen fortunes of Greek church embroidery at the turn of the

[50] Victoria and Albert Museum, Early Christian and Byzantine Art, 1955, pl. 28.

seventeenth and eighteenth centuries, had too fine a taste to overload her compositions with excessive ornament, but shared the feeling of her period for the purely
pretty. Her decoration was elegant, delicately coloured and finely worked. She
was fond of pearls and also used coloured stones with careful restraint. She,
and many of her followers, used floral scroll borders, and she sometimes also   **46, 114**
borrowed ornamental motifs from Italy, in the same way that she drew on Italian   **55**
iconography in an attempt to renew the artistic poverty of the embroideries of her
time. Her epitaphioi in particular had little formal decoration, but relied on
decorative details in the haloes and in the traditional sun, moon and stars which
powdered the background. In her hands the stars were once again reduced to
reasonable numbers and proportions, and ceased to overwhelm the figures as they
had come to do in the preceding centuries. Epitaphioi had for a long time had
virtually no background ornament but stars, largely because the elaboration of the
iconography left little room for anything else. This became increasingly true
during the seventeenth century, and Despoineta's wide plain backgrounds appear
to have been a deliberate reaction against this tendency. In one sense her rejection
of formal ornament (which is found only in her epitaphioi since her other
embroideries are quite heavily decorated), could be said to parallel the severer
style of the mid-sixteenth century, but comparison of one of Despoineta's
characteristic haloes with haloes of the earlier period will serve to underline the
completely different approach.

The prettiness of Despoineta's work was echoed by many of her followers
(the icon of the Nun Agatha is a good example). The floral border, however,   **75**
continued in popularity through the eighteenth century. One piece in particular,
the epitaphios of Theodosia Kasymbouri, made for a monastery at Trebizond,   **116**
seems to reflect in its decoration, both in the elaborate border and in isolated
flowers in the ground, the Persian-based style of the Three Hierarchs embroideries
made almost exactly a hundred years earlier. Very many eighteenth century
pieces show the influence of Turkish flower embroidery in their borders, or, in
the case of some aëres, consist entirely of Asia Minor flower patterns.

Another designer who made use of the traditional flowers of Turkish decoration — the rose, the carnation and the tulip — was the Serb, Christopher
Žefarović, who worked in the north of Serbia towards the middle of the eighteenth
century. The wide floral borders on the two podeai made for the Brăncoveanu   **73**
family go farther in naturalism and the abandonment of formal pattern than anything in the style which preceded them.

At the same time Žefarović's connections with Vienna introduced him to the
European baroque, and his epitaphioi are framed in heavy borders of baroque   **119**
acanthus ornament, a fashion which was taken up and copied in the north for the
rest of the century.

Stoles of the seventeenth and eighteenth centuries relied almost without exception on architectural arcading as a framework. This became increasingly more elaborate as time went on. The arch became wider, and at the same time architecturally more improbable, as the vestment widened. The eighteenth century stole is typified by those designed by Žefarović. With their wide arches and massive gold ornament they are a far cry from the first plain arcades of the fifteenth century.

47

Figure **a**	҂З̄	=	7000	
Figure **b**	ꙃ̄ ҂ѕ̄	=	6000	
Figure **c** }	҂З̄Ч̄Є̄	=	7000 : 90 : 5	} 7095
	О̄Ч̄Є̄	=	70 : 90 : 5	
Figure **d**	҂а̄Х̄п̄З̄	=	1687 (from Christ)	
Figure **e** }	҂З̄Є̄І̄	=	7000 : 5 : 10	} 7015
	҂З̄І̄Є̄	=	7000 : 10 : 5	

Figures **a** *to* **e.** (*see page* 51)

48

CHAPTER SIX

INSCRIPTIONS

Needlework is not usually regarded as the best medium for the reproduction of the written word, since the embroidering of letters in any of the many possible techniques is a slow process requiring extreme exactitude in a very small space. This is even more true of gold embroidery than of other methods. Embroiderers in the Orthodox church, however, seem to have taken quite long inscriptions for granted, and invariably worked them throughout in gold thread.[51] Why this should have been so is not very clear. Dedicatory inscriptions were a commonplace in the Byzantine arts, but often seem to have been less elaborate, even when the medium employed would have presented fewer difficulties in the working.

These inscriptions are frequently treated as part of the design, usually as a border on a veil, or as a panel at the bottom of a stole. If the lettering is carried out with elegance, as it very often is, the inscription itself can be extremely decorative, and in some cases provides almost the only ornament in the whole composition. This is particularly true of the Slavonic inscriptions of the late fifteenth and early sixteenth centuries, where the lettering has obviously been influenced by Kufic **79** script and, like many Arabic inscriptions, is used as much for decoration as for information.

This is not always so, however, and many inscriptions are crudely lettered **42** and badly arranged. It is clear that the embroiderers, and perhaps the designers as well, were often illiterate. In later work especially, there are frequent mistakes in spelling and grammar. Nor do embroiderers, even those whose finished inscriptions provide a pleasing decorative border at first glance, ever seem to have mastered the art of spacing their lettering. Words were run together, or broken to fit a line without reference to the spelling, and the practice by which the writers of Greek and Slavonic manuscripts habitually made use of abbreviations and contractions to produce an accepted form of shorthand was carried to extremes, so that quite long names were often represented by only two or three letters.

[51] Lettering worked in silk on the St. Mark's altar cloth is a restoration.

All this, especially when it is aggravated by wear and tear, does not make for easy reading, but apart from these hazards, the Byzantine scholar will naturally understand the inscriptions and have no further need of explanations. The aim of this chapter is simply to give the amateur a general idea of their content.

In the earlier embroideries two languages are involved, Greek and Old Slavonic. Both are written in approximately the same alphabet, that is the Greek alphabet of the Middle Ages, with some additions for Slavonic sounds which do not occur in Greek.

When the Slav tribes settled in the Balkan peninsula in the course of the sixth century all spoke roughly the same language, although with local dialects, but it was not until the ninth century that a written language was developed, in the first instance for the use of the church. Constantine the Philosopher of Salonica, later known as St. Cyril, and his brother Methodius were the first missionaries to the Slavs, and Constantine is regarded as responsible for the invention of two Slavonic alphabets, Cyrillic and Glagolitic. The first is basically the Greek alphabet with certain additions. The second is much more cumbersome, and only remotely allied to any other alphabet. One theory suggests that St. Cyril first devised Cyrillic for the use of the Slav peoples round Salonica and later invented Glagolitic when he and his brother were sent as missionaries to Moravia in 862. Another regards Glagolitic as his first invention and holds that it was superseded by the simpler Cyrillic during the eleventh and twelfth centuries. However this may have been, Cyrillic had come to be the alphabet of all the Slav languages by this period, Glagolitic surviving only for church use among the Slav Catholics of Dalmatia and Croatia. As far as the embroideries are concerned therefore, the two alphabets we have to deal with are medieval Greek and Cyrillic which, as we have seen, closely resemble each other.[52] The modern Greek alphabet has been revised and is now much nearer to the classical form. Cyrillic, with adaptions and simplifications in the lettering, remains the alphabet of modern Russia, Serbia and Bulgaria. The medieval alphabet is given at Appendix 2, with English transliteration and modern Greek.

After the deaths of St. Cyril and St. Methodius their disciples moved into Bulgaria and Macedonia, where St. Clement and St. Naum carried on from Ochrid the work of founding schools and monasteries, translating the scriptures and developing the Slav liturgy. In this way the old Slav language, Old Slavonic or Church Slavonic, became the language of the church in all the Orthodox countries of the Balkans, and remained so even though the spoken language was

[52] A strong argument against the so-called Purse of St. Stephen in the Schatzkammer in Vienna ever having belonged to St. Stephen of Hungary, who died in 1038, is the fact that the inscriptions are in Cyrillic. Had it been made in his lifetime, especially in Pannonia, the inscriptions must have been in Glagolitic. See Mirković, Crkveni Umetnički Vez, pp. 45-8.

considerably modified in different countries. Slavonic was also used by the church in Rumania, which was originally converted by Slav missionaries, but where the language of the people is not Slav but Latin-based.

Inscriptions on embroideries from all the Balkan countries and Rumania were normally in Church Slavonic, or sometimes in Slavonic and Greek, but by the seventeenth century Slavonic began to be replaced by the everyday language of the country concerned, especially when the actual text of the Liturgy was not involved. From this time on, therefore, there are inscriptions in Serb and Russian, and such curiosities as Rumanian inscriptions written in Cyrillic characters.

The Orthodox church traditionally reckoned dates from the assumed year of the Creation, calculated as 5508 years before the birth of Christ. To arrive at the western equivalent, therefore, this figure must be subtracted from the date given, i.e., 7095 —5508 = 1587.[53] Numbers, in both Greek and Slavonic, were shown by the normal Greek method of using letters of the alphabet. The classical Greek alphabet of twenty-four letters was just too short to provide symbols, counted in digits, tens and hundreds, for every numeral up to 900. Three symbols were therefore introduced into the Greek alphabet in Alexandrian times which were used solely as numerals. They had no place in the written language. These were the *digamma* (later *stigma*), *koppa* and *sampi*, which respectively stood for 6, 90 and 900. The same figures were represented in Old Slavonic by Slavonic characters not used in Greek. In addition Slavonic retained the Greek *thita* for 9, although this letter was not necessary to reproduce a Slavonic consonant. Corresponding letters and figures are also given at Appendix 2.

All numbers were indicated (or should have been) by a line over the top of the letter. The thousands were shown by the digit letter with a small stroke in front (fig. **a**). This stroke sometimes looks as if it is attached to the letter and can produce a confusing outline (fig. **b**). Most embroiderers seem to have been clear about the placing of numerals, so that 7095 should read seven thousand: ninety: five, but such deviations as seventy: ninety: five are not unknown (fig. **c**). In Slavonic, but not in Greek, it was correct to reverse the tens and digit figures for numbers from 11 to 19 (fig. **e**). Again by the seventeenth century, it is not unusual to find a date reckoned from Christ instead of from the Creation, but still in letters (fig. **d**) or quite simply reckoned from Christ and written in Latin numerals.

The word indiction (ἡ ἴνδικτος, ἡ ἰνδικτιών) under the Byzantine Empire described a fifteen year period relating to tax collection. The system, which was first instituted by Diocletian, was revised by Constantine and the first fifteen year

---

[53] The year was reckoned from the 1st September. Strictly speaking 5508 should be deducted from 1st January to 31st August, and 5509 from 1st September to 31st December, but embroideries are seldom dated so accurately.

indiction ran from September 312.[54] The same word followed by a figure indicated a particular year in any given period of fifteen years, but did not by itself of course constitute a date. Although the system was widely used in public decrees and official documents, an indiction number on an embroidery is rare. **99** One occurs on the Nicholas Eudaimonoioannes epitaphios.

Inscriptions fall into three distinct categories. There are the short titles which identify by name a saint or scene, there are quotations from the scriptures or the Liturgy, and there are the dedicatory inscriptions which name the donor and sometimes the church to which the gift was made.

The labelling of scenes and figures dated from the period when the church laid particular emphasis on teaching the scriptures by artistic illustration. The tradition was strengthened after the iconoclast period when those who brought back the icons were at pains to clarify the relationship between holy picture and beholder, and wished to identify without room for doubt the saint whose Christian attributes were reflected in the painted image. The Orthodox church has preserved this tradition to the present day, and never adopted to any great extent the western system of identifying saints by symbols.

Even in countries where Old Slavonic was the normal language of the church, the traditional Greek names were often used for saints and scenes, so that it is quite normal to find an embroidery with Greek titles and a dedication in Slavonic. This applied particularly to the traditional Greek monograms for Christ and the Virgin Mary. Some common monograms and contractions are given at fig. **f**.

In addition to the titles, which are simply for identification, many embroideries also have quotations from scripture, and more often from the poetic hymns which form so rich a part of the Orthodox liturgy. Many of them date back to Byzantine times. It is of course impossible to give all these quotations, and the following are only a few examples.

Thus we find on a stole, ' And when they had bound Him they led Him away and delivered Him to Pilate the Governor ', (Matt. 27, 2), which refers to the symbolic meaning attached to the epitrachilion (see p. 17). On epimanikia we occasionally find the verses from the Psalms which the priest recites as he vests himself, ' Thy hands have made me and fashioned me ' (Ps. 119, 73), and ' The right hand of the Lord hath exalted me: the right hand of the Lord doeth valiantly ' **85, 86** (Ps. 118, 16). Very frequently on aëres are the words of the Communion, ' Take, eat, this is my Body ', and ' Drink ye all of this, this is my Blood '. If the Evangelists or the Early Fathers are shown carrying scrolls, the quotation on the scroll is from the beginning of the appropriate Gospel or from a prayer connected with the Hierarch in question, for example for St. John the Evangelist, ' In the

---

[54] V. Grumel, Traité d'Etudes Byzantines I, La Chronologie, 1958, p. 192.

IC XC	Ἰησοῦς Χριστός	Jesus Christ
MP ΘΫ	Μήτηρ Θεοῦ	The Mother of God
ὁ ΑΓ	ὁ ἅγιος	(Greek)
		Saint
CTЪ CTH	Sveti	(Slavonic)
ὁ ΑΡΧ ΓΑΒ	ὁ Ἀρχάγγελος Γαβριήλ	The Archangel Gabriel
ΑΓΓΕΛΟC ΚΫ	ὁ Ἄγγελος Κυρίου	
ΑΓΓΕΚΫ	The Angel of the Lord	
IC XC NK	Ἰησοῦς Χριστός Νικᾶ	Jesus Christ conquers
ΦΧΦΠ	Φῶς Χριστοῦ Φάινει Πᾶσιν	The Light of Christ shines for all
Φ ZⱲH C	Φῶς, Ζωή	Light, Life
O ⱲN		He that is

Figure f.   (see page 52).

beginning was the Word and the Word was God '. A paraphrase of Luke 23, 42 is often used by donors as part of the dedication, ' Remember me, Lord, in Thy Kingdom '.

Quotations from the Liturgy and from the hymns, or troparia, for Good Friday and Holy Saturday are often used at some length on epitaphioi. Among the most common are one or more verses from the troparion for Good Friday evening, a hymn to St. Joseph of Arimathea:

> The honourable Joseph, having taken down Thy undefiled Body from the Cross and wrapped it in a clean linen cloth with sweet-smelling herbs, laid it with funeral rites in a new tomb.
>
> Glory. When thou, the undying Life, camest down to death, thou didst overcome Hell through the lightning of the Godhead. When thou didst raise the dead from the underworld all the powers of Heaven cried: Glory be to thee, the giver of Life, O Christ our Lord.
>
> To the spice-bearing women the angel standing by the tomb cried, Spices are fitting for mortal men but Christ has been shown a stranger to corruption.

The troparion for the morning of Holy Saturday is very long and is sung in the form of statement and answer, as in a litany. Two of the most frequently quoted verses are the following:

> Thou Christ, the Life, wast laid in the grave, and the hosts of angels were amazed, glorifying thy descent.
>
> Thou, the Life, how canst thou die? How live in the grave? Thou hast destroyed the kingdom of death and raised up the dead from Hell.

Another quotation from the Liturgy which is very often used is the invocation known as the Trisagion:

> O Holy God, O Holy Mighty, O Holy Immortal, have mercy upon us.

Many, or even most, embroidered vestments appear to have been offered as gifts to churches and monasteries by individuals, on an occasion important either to the church concerned or to the donor personally. Many of the donors recorded their names and sometimes the date of their gift, asking at the same time for forgiveness of their sins, for divine grace for themselves and their families, or for God's mercy on the soul of a departed relative.

The change in social conditions between the Byzantine and Turkish periods is reflected in the rank of the donors. In Byzantine times it was the aristocracy who commissioned embroideries. A few are known to have been the gifts of Byzantine emperors. Other inscriptions name noblemen and high officials of church and state. Many embroideries were the offerings of ruling princes in Serbia and the Rumanian principalities.

With the coming of the Turks the aristocracy was gradually eliminated, except in the Rumanian principalities. Eventually a bourgeois class of rich merchants became the leaders of Christian communities under the Turkish officials, and it was they who offered most of the embroideries. At the same time it became quite common for the lower ranks in the ecclesiastical hierarchy to give them as well.

85, 86 One of the most elaborate dedications is on the pair of Communion veils at Halberstadt, which read as follows:

> If no Israelite might look directly upon the countenance of Moses when he came from the mountain where he had seen God, how shall I look upon Thy revered Body unveiled, how regard it? I fear to offer it these trifles, Thou, Lord of all (earthly) things, I, Thy pious servant, Sebastos Alexios Palaiologos. But grant, by Thy Grace, O Word, that at the Day of Judgement I may look on Thy countenance.

And on the other:

> An adulteress offered Thee tears and ointment. Having dried Thy feet with her hair she received at once forgiveness of her sins. But I have nothing of this kind. For tears I bring Thee pearls, for ointment I offer gold, O Word, and instead of hair I bring Thee this cloth, I who would reverently touch Thy Mysteries, Sebastos Alexios Palaiologos, who asks forgiveness of his countless sins.

For the most part, however, the language is much less flowery. A very typical Moldavian dedication comes from the Stephen the Great epitaphios given to Moldoviţa:

> By the will of the Father, the aid of the Son and the operation of the Holy Spirit, John Stephen, Voivod, by the Grace of God ruler of Moldavia, son of Voivod Bogdan, with his devout wife Maria and his well-loved sons, Alexander and Bogdan-Vlad, made this veil at the monastery of Moldoviţa where there is the church of the Annunciation to the Holy Mother of God, in the year 7002, March 30th.

Others are even shorter, for example, on an orarion in the Victoria and Albert Museum:

48
> John Peter Voivod and his son Mark Voivod in the year 7046.

Dedications in Slavonic, such as the one by Stephen the Great above, normally used the word ' sŭtvori ', literally ' created (by) ', but since it was used by princes, priests and court officials alike, it is quite clear that it should be read in the sense of ' caused to be made '. Even when the donor was a woman, it does not follow that she ' created ' the vestment with her own hands.

Sometimes a dedication ends by calling down a curse on anyone who shall remove the vestment from the church to which it has been given, as in the case of Euphemia's curtain at Chilandari. A Rumanian epitrachilion[55] provides a supreme example of the inability of embroiderers to manage the lay-out of their lettering. The inscription carries the first half of the warning against removing it, but has to omit for lack of space the horrid penalties that would attend this act.

Two known embroideries consist entirely of a written inscription. One of these is an embroidered copy of a famous piece of Serbian medieval poetry, the

[55] Mirković, Crkveni Umetnički Vez, p. 42.

Laud to Prince Lazar, written by Euphemia, widow of the Despot Uglješ, after 78 Lazar's death at the battle of Kossovo (see p. 58 below). The other is a copy of 77 the Nicene Creed in Greek.

Secular and ecclesiastical ranks used by donors to describe themselves are often confusing to western readers. It may therefore be helpful to explain some of the titles most often met with in inscriptions.

SECULAR

Sevastocrator	High-ranking titles of the Byzantine aristocracy
Sevastos	
Despot	Before the Turkish conquest a prince or high-ranking noble ruling important territories in Byzantium or Serbia. After the conquest, the prince of Serbia ruling as a vassal of the Sultan.
Voivod	A ruling prince of Moldavia or Wallachia
Župan	An aristocratic rank in Serbia
Boyar	A nobleman in Rumania or Bulgaria
Hetman	Military commander-in-chief

The following were court officials to a ruling prince or great land owner:

Great Logothete	High Chancellor
Vistiernik	Treasurer
Dvornik	An official at the court representing the affairs of a particular province
Stolnik } *These became honorary titles*	Steward, who looked after the catering and kitchens
Žitničer }	Overseer of crops

ECCLESIASTIC

Patriarch, Archbishop and Bishop (Archiepiscopos, Episcopos) will need no explanation. A Metropolitan in the Orthodox church is in charge of a district and ranks higher than an Archbishop.

IN MONASTIC LIFE

Higoumenos	Abbot of a monastery
Monachos (f. monachi)	Monk, nun
Hieromonachos	A monk who has been ordained priest

We find embroideries given by ecclesiastics who describe themselves by rank and as being ' of the Great Church ' (τῆς Μεγάλης Ἐκκλησίας), that is the Patriarchate at Constantinople. These are officials of the Patriarch's entourage, among whom are: the Great Steward (Οἰκονόμος), the Great Logothete (Λογοθέτης), Chartophylax (Χαρτοφύλαξ), Skevophylax (Σκευοφύλαξ), Syngellos (Συγγέλλος), and Sakellarios (Σακελλάριος).

CHAPTER SEVEN

WORKERS AND WORKROOMS

The anonymity which has effectively hidden every trace of the individual Byzantine artist has been put down to the low social status of the working artist/craftsman, who was rated no higher than the artisan.[56]   The same author suggests that Orthodox artists first started to sign their work in the sixteenth and seventeenth centuries under the influence of the much higher social position accorded to the artist by the Venetians.   As far as embroidery is concerned, no trace has survived of the workers of the Byzantine period.   We do not know any of their names, nor how or where they worked.[57]   Nor is it at all easy on evidence of style or iconography to associate different schools with different places.

We can, however, make some reasonable assumptions.   A certain amount of rather fragmentary evidence indicates the pattern in England at this period. Here the work was evidently done both in the monasteries and in secular workrooms and by both men and women.   Some of their names are known, not it must be admitted because any of them signed their work, but largely through accounts of payments made to them.   These men and women were professionals, and although only one name may be mentioned as the recipient of a fee, it must be assumed that this person did not work alone but ran a workroom.

Similar evidence does not appear to exist in the case of Byzantium, but it is probably safe to suppose that all the important medieval gold embroideries were worked in much the same circumstances.   The strict craft guild system in force in Constantinople would have precluded mention of individuals.   In fact, nothing seems to be known of any guild of embroiderers,[58] but it can be taken for granted that there were always professional embroiderers working in the city.   The fact that there are no records of their organisation into a guild suggests that in early centuries their work was considered relatively unimportant, and further, that they

---

[56] G. Mathew, Byzantine Aesthetics, p. 25.

[57] The only exception is the Syropoulos epitaphios, the dating of which remains very much open to doubt (see p. 80 below).   Even so we know nothing of Syropoulos but his name.

[58] J. Ebersolt, Les arts somptuaires de Byzance, 1923, Chap. I.

formed a subsidiary branch of another guild, for example, the weavers, workers in gold, or even the clothiers.

It is clear from the inscriptions that very many or indeed most of these embroideries were commissioned by individuals as gifts to the church, and the work was obviously carried out in professional workrooms, whether secular or monastic. In the Byzantine period the embroideries were the expensive gifts of wealthy personages, and the work put into them involved a high degree of professional expertise. Whether a workroom was run outside the church as the appendage of a court, or under the auspices of a monastery, the professional attitude to the work and the technical requirements must have been the same. It must be remembered that the Byzantine monastery existed principally to bear witness to the holy life through prayer and intercession, and it seems likely that, at any rate in Constantinople itself, embroidery was made in the imperial workrooms.

After the Turkish occupation monasteries certainly helped to preserve the craft, and many of the signed pieces of the sixteenth and seventeenth centuries were made by monks and nuns. The question whether there were ever embroidery workrooms in the monasteries of Mount Athos remains open. The traditional artistic crafts were icon painting, illumination and wood carving, and no trace of a tradition of embroidery seems to have survived. A large number of the embroideries preserved on the Holy Mountain were gifts to the monasteries from outside. Others have nothing to show their origin, and may or may not have been made on the spot.

There is also the question whether any of the embroideries were made by the aristocratic ladies whose names appear in the inscriptions. Some authorities have taken it for granted that if a woman was named as the donor, she did the embroidery herself, but as a general rule it must be assumed that this was not so, especially in the early period. Gold embroidery on this scale and of this standard is a highly professional skill, acquired only by long practice as an apprentice. It is not impossible that the individual princess should have achieved this expertise, but it is very unlikely that many of them did. We have seen already that the wording of the inscriptions, especially in Slavonic, often stated that a piece was ' made by ' the donor, but it is safe to say that this should never be read literally.

In later centuries some work, although by no means all, does have a very amateurish appearance, and may either have been done in small convents where standards were not high, or by individuals.

Two ladies who enjoy a traditional reputation as embroideresses were the Serbian princess Euphemia, and Maria of Mangop, second of the three wives of Stephen the Great of Moldavia.

Euphemia was married to the Despot Uglješ of Serbia, who was killed at the battle of the Maritsa in 1371. As a widow she took refuge at the court of Prince

58

Lazar of Serbia, but in 1389 he too was killed at Kossovo, the disastrous defeat which finally delivered Serbia to Turkish suzerainty. After the battle Euphemia and Lazar's widow, Milica, took the veil together. Euphemia composed the poem for which her name has remained famous, the Laud to Prince Lazar, extolling her fallen prince and lamenting the fate of her country. She also travelled widely in the train of the widowed Queen Milica. Both were eventually buried at the convent of Ljubostinje.

Her name is connected with three embroideries, a pall for Prince Lazar's coffin, intended to cover the face only, on which the text of the Laud is worked with no other ornament but a narrow border, an iconostasis curtain for the Athonite monastery of Chilandari where her son was a monk, and the epitaphios at Putna inscribed by Euphemia and Eupraxia. Whether Euphemia herself had any hand in the actual embroidering of these works is open to doubt. For one thing it may be supposed that her role as companion to Milica left her little time. For another all these pieces, the curtain especially, show a highly professional skill in design and technique. Certainly it may be said that she encouraged the Serbian workrooms of this difficult period with her interest and patronage, but Kossovo had virtually brought to an end the great period of Serbian church embroidery.

Little more than half a century later Constantinople itself fell to the Turks, and it was left to Moldavia to provide the civilised and wealthy background necessary before such a luxury craft could flourish. The monasteries which Stephen the Great, as an enlightened and deeply religious ruler, founded in his kingdom received many gifts of embroidered vestments from him, and his second and third wives, both called Maria, are frequently mentioned with him in the inscriptions. Church embroidery was made in Moldavia in the time of Stephen's predecessors, but undoubtedly reached its greatest heights during his reign, so that there is some ground for the theory which connects Maria of Mangop with the craft. She was the daughter of a Byzantine family named Theodoros, who during the fifteenth century held a small independent dukedom based on the fortress of Mangop in the Crimea. They appear to have been related to the Comneni in Trebizond, and through Maria's mother to the Palaeologi. All travellers to Mangop have agreed on the magnificence of its churches and palaces, and speak of such things as walls covered with mosaics, which suggest a high degree of Byzantine luxury.[59] This would obviously have included embroidered vestments in the churches, so that Maria must have been familiar with them, but whether her role was simply that of patroness to Stephen's workrooms, or whether, as some authorities suggest, she was herself a highly accomplished needlewoman, must remain a matter for conjecture. It must be remembered that she died in 1477 after only five years

[59] N. Banescu, La seigneury de Théodoro—Mangoup en Crimée, BZ XXXV, 1935.

in Moldavia, and it seems more likely that her real contribution was to bring workers from her father's court who established the tradition at Putna. The most famous of the embroideries associated with Maria is the funerary portrait on her own tomb cover.

The names of several other Rumanian princesses have been connected with embroideries, among them Despina, the Serbian wife of Neagoe Basarab, Voivod of Wallachia in the early years of the sixteenth century, and Helena, also Serbian by birth, the wife of Peter Rareş of Moldavia in the middle of the same century. At the beginning of the seventeenth century Marguita, the wife of Simeon Movila, gave a number of embroideries to the monastery of Suceviţa. It seems a safe assumption that all of these were the donors rather than the embroideresses of their gifts.

If we are to accept Mirković's dating of the Syropoulos epitaphios at Chilandari (see p. 80 below) this is by far the earliest piece to be signed without any doubt by the worker. Even if we accept Mirković's attribution to the monastery of Lesnovo, but because of the iconography and apparent technical style, assume that the presentation was made well after the consecration of the church, the veil must be dated to the middle of the fifteenth century, and Syropoulos must still have been one of the earliest to sign his work.

From the second half of the sixteenth century onwards signed work is quite usual, especially in Greece and Yugoslavia. It seems to have been less common in Rumania. The worker is clearly indicated in the inscriptions by the words ' the work of . . . ', ' the labour of . . . ', or ' by the hand of . . . '. For the most part nothing more is known of these workers than the single name on one, or occasionally two or three, embroideries. There is, for example, the Nun Agni who signed the mid-sixteenth century curtain now in the Museum of Decorative Art in Belgrade; Alexandra Dena, who appears to have worked in the west of Greece at the end of the sixteenth century, and has left three signed works, one of which is a cuff in the Victoria and Albert Museum;[60] the monk Arsenius, who has left two epitaphioi from the same period; and the nun Philothea of Constantinople, who signed the epitaphios dated 1608 at Secu. These are only a few of many known names. A list of workers is given in the Catalogue of Church Embroideries in the Benaki Museum.

Some embroideries of the sixteenth and seventeenth centuries, especially from the Rumanian principalities, form small groups which obviously came from the same workrooms. Much the most important of these consists of the later embroideries from Stephen the Great's monastery at Putna, which at the end of the fifteenth and beginning of the sixteenth centuries produced a series of hangings which have a real artistic and technical homogeneity. Apart from these, some

[60] Victoria and Albert Museum, Early Christian and Byzantine Art, 1955, pl. 28.

others can be linked by their ornament but not assigned to any particular designer or workroom.   There is, for example, a group of mid-sixteenth century stoles from Moldavia, and two Wallachian oraria of the same period, while a third, more important, group is formed by the embroideries from Jassy of the 1630's.   These last were presumably made in the town.   Embroiderers of this period who signed their work have either not left enough for special characteristics to become apparent, or have followed the traditional methods so closely that they have not formed an individual style.   Not until the last years of the seventeenth century do we find an embroideress who can be said to have founded a ' school ' in the artistic sense.

Despoineta, whose signed work is dated from 1682 to 1723, describes herself as the daughter of Argyris, and on one work gives the district of Constantinople where she lived.   Eleven of her signed works exist, as well as several pieces attributed to her workroom, and two signed by pupils who mention her name.   These are Euphrosyne, who worked an icon of St. Nicholas in the Benaki Museum, and Alexandra, who is mentioned with Despoineta as the worker of an epitaphios dated 1712 in the Victoria and Albert Museum, and worked another epitaphios, now in the treasury of the theological college on the island of Heybeli (Halkí), under her supervision in 1714.

Despoineta appears to have been aware that church embroidery had exhausted the artistic possibilities of its Byzantine origins, and to have turned deliberately to the west for fresh inspiration.   Her handling of the Adoration of the Magi in the epigonation illustrated is recognisably western, and her technical treatment of faces and other flesh parts, for which she used shading in curiously dark tones of gold-coloured silk rather than the traditional linear drawing of features, is very reminiscent of Italian work.   Since there was a considerable Italian colony in Constantinople at this time, it is possible that she had the opportunity to see both Italian pictures and needlework.   In spite of this leaning towards an Italian style she seems to have made only very tentative efforts to render perspective.   Her characterisation of figures was excellent, and more naturally emotional than the rather stylised expression of mourning which the Byzantine Lamentation had become by the seventeenth century.   She evidently had a fondness for the purely pretty, and used pale coloured silks for her floral borders, as well as pearls and coloured stones.   Her distinctive manner of working haloes in a star pattern was in keeping with her love of ornamental effect.

This Greek woman who lived, as she herself tells us, by the Double Pillars[61] in Turkish Istanbul, was an artist and a very gifted embroideress.   Her work has a true elegance of style as well as great decorative charm.   She was one of the very

[61] The quay called the Double Columns was at the southern outlet of the Bosphorus where the Palace of Dolma Bahçe now stands. (S. Runciman, The Fall of Constantinople 1453, 1965, p. 219.)

few designers who introduced a sense of innovation and original thought to Orthodox church embroidery, and there is no doubt that she inspired a considerable following among Greek workers during the next hundred years. Among her immediate successors we have the Nun Agatha, whose icon of St. George is illustrated, and a worker called Mariora, who left five signed works, but about whom we have no other information. Kokona[62] tou Rologa, who signed four pieces, one of which is the epitaphios of 1829 illustrated at pl. 118, was obviously still influenced by Despoineta's treatment of the Lamentation, but compared to Despoineta her work is coarse and her characterisation shows the excessive sentimentality which disfigured the embroideries of the nineteenth century.

In the 1730's we find a workroom run in Trebizond by Theodosia the daughter of Kasymbouri, who, like Despoineta, mentions the name of a pupil, Elizabeth, on her surviving epitaphios. Theodosia's only known works are the epitaphios from the famous monastery of Soumelá at Trebizond, and an icon of St. George from the Cathedral of Argyropolis, both now in the Benaki Museum. The inscription on the latter actually states that the work was done in Trebizond.

Theodosia's work has all the rich decorative effect common to the eighteenth century. As well as an elaborate floral border, her epitaphios has elegant single flowers scattered on the 'grass' below the bier, which are certainly copied from Persian silks. Iconographically her Lamentation is rather old-fashioned, and it is not artistically successful. The space is badly crowded and an attempt to put the angels and the bier in perspective has led to a confusion of arms and wings, while a dispossessed hand, presumably belonging to the Magdalene, appears awkwardly over the Virgin's head. Theodosia was nevertheless an excellent embroideress, who was certainly influenced technically by Despoineta and may even have been a pupil of hers. She uses Despoineta's star-patterned haloes, and her treatment of faces and flesh is also in the Italianate style. In spite of the clumsy drawing, the epitaphios creates the impression of a very fine piece of embroidery.

While Despoineta's influence remained paramount in Greece and Asia Minor throughout the eighteenth century, another well-known designer developed a rather different style in the north of Serbia. Rather more is known about the life of Christopher Žefarović than about most embroidery designers, largely because of his work as an engraver. He was born in Macedonia towards the end of the seventeenth century and took holy orders. During the 1730's he came, as an artist already trained and established, to work under the auspices of the Orthodox Archbishop of Karlovci. These lands north of the Danube, which had been settled by Serbs escaping from the Turkish occupation, were at that time under

[62] Kokóna, kokonítsa, like despoina, despoineta, means Miss, young lady, or 'little miss', and like Despoineta was used as a Christian name. A number of eighteenth century embroideries are signed Kokóna, followed by the father's name.

the jurisdiction of the Habsburg Empire, which allowed the Patriarchate of Karlovci a reasonable autonomy, so that it became one of the chief centres of the Orthodox faith in the Balkans. The see nevertheless had a difficult role between the Turks on the one hand and Roman Catholic propaganda on the other, and it was in this situation that Žefarović's talents as an artist were put to good use by his Archbishop. During the 1740's he visited Vienna, where he appears to have studied engraving under Thomas Mesmer, and it was he who introduced this art to Serbia. His engravings, made in the service of his church, are all religious and patriotic in character, and are strongly influenced by the extravagant spirit of the Viennese baroque.

His embroidery designs all date from the last years of his life. Some of them were definitely carried out in Vienna, and it is possible that all his embroideries were worked there. The technical standards are extremely high, and it is in any case most unlikely that he was himself the embroiderer. He can, for one reason, hardly have had the time. His existing signed works include three epitaphioi, a saccos, two curtains, two large podeai and seven stoles. He died on a visit to Russia in 1753.

15, 47
71-74
119

Unlike Despoineta, whose object was to simplify the elaboration which began to load the iconography of the Lamentation during the seventeenth century, Žefarović carried this tendency to the farthest possible extreme. Every figure mentioned in the Gospel accounts of the Crucifixion as a friend of Jesus is gathered round the bier, the angels have left their liturgical role as guardians of the Holy Mystery and mingle with the crowd. The Evangelists in decorative frames, the Cross, the Instruments of the Passion, the vessels for the oils, seraphim and cherubim, sun and moon and hanging lamps all fill the background, and room is found on top of all this for small architectural scenes of Jersulaem, Gethsemane and Golgotha. The whole is surrounded by an elaborate border of acanthus leaves in the baroque style. The wonder is that Žefarović managed to unite all these details into a homogeneous whole and even to achieve a certain elegance in his compositions.

These embroideries appear to be the first examples in the Orthodox church to abandon the Byzantine insistence on metal threads. Only the stoles are worked in the traditional gold and silver. In the other embroideries the figures are worked throughout in coloured silk, and gold is confined to decoration and such details as haloes and lamps. There is also a distinctive manner of working haloes in a couched pattern of curving rays, which are sometimes studded with rosette-like flowers. These rays were not a Byzantine pattern, but were often used by embroiderers in Germany and the Low Countries in the late middle ages. Embroidery in coloured silk used in imitation of painting was of course a commonplace in the west long before the middle of the eighteenth century, but in eastern Europe outside Russia it was an entirely new departure from tradition. It enabled the worker of the door curtain of the Vision of Ezekiel to achieve a degree of perspective drawing which had never before been attempted in Orthodox church embroidery. Both this technique and the halo patterns may well have been due to the Viennese workroom rather than to Žefarović as a designer.

On the other hand the combination of the elegant naturalistic roses, tulips and carnations of Turkish flower decoration with rich baroque patterns which he used to make important borders and frames for his work were probably of his own design. Similar border patterns occur in many of his engravings. There is no evidence to show whether he had an opportunity to see the highly decorative Rumanian embroideries of the preceding century, although he executed several commissions for the boyar families of Wallachia, but his designs are certainly in sympathy with the fashion of his time for lavish floral settings.

Another baroque designer who must surely have seen Žefarović's work and been influenced by him, was Marina Ruelandt or Ruheland, who worked in the last years of the eighteenth century. Nothing is known of her except the signature on two epitaphioi, one of which was once in Eger, in Hungary, the other dedicated to a church in Joannina. Mirković suggests, credibly enough taking into account the style of her work and the form of the inscriptions, that she may have lived in Budapest or Vienna, where there were Greek communities.[63] Her name would seem to indicate a Greek mother and a German father, or perhaps Greek parents and a German husband. The epitaphios dated 1800, illustrated by Mirković, follows Žefarović's iconography and decorative effects very closely, even to the flower rosettes on the haloes, but like Kokona tou Rologa, her figures already have a nineteenth century sentimentality of expression and gesture.

Žefarović appears to have had other, less talented copyists. An epitaphios in Cyprus, dated 1792[64] has the same haloes, and much of the background detail, particularly the treatment of cherubim and seraphim, seems to have been copied direct from Žefarović's Bucharest epitaphios. The ornate border is also in his style, although it is a poor imitation. An attempt has been made to put the bier in perspective by placing it at an angle, but the group is both sentimental and clumsy.

Despoineta and Žefarović were the last designers to produce work of any artistic merit. In their different spheres they brought about a genuine revival in these embroideries during the first half of the eighteenth century, but this impetus did not last beyond their immediate followers.

---

[63] Mirković, Crkveni Umetnički Vez, p. 26. Pl. VIII/1.
[64] M. Beza, Byzantine Art in Roumania, Pl. 20.

CHAPTER EIGHT

TECHNIQUE

The difficulty of defining precisely in modern technical language the various words used by Byzantine writers to describe gold-decorated stuffs has already been mentioned, and it is not lessened by the obvious fact that most of the writers had themselves no exact knowledge of the processes they were describing, and used various expressions in a very general sense which merely indicated that the finished material had a golden appearance. Angeliki Hadjimichaeli[65] has made a spirited attempt to sort out this confusion, but it seems likely that precise definitions will never be achieved, possibly because the terms used had themselves no precise meaning. Those who are interested will find in her article a list of the Greek words used by Byzantine writers in connection with gold-decorated textiles.

The fascination that gold held for the Byzantines may have been due to a hard-headed admiration for its basic worth, or aesthetic appreciation of its colour and its unique ability to hold and reflect, almost to embody light. Certainly their preoccupation with the glory of gold in all its forms lasted several hundred years and was allied to a very strong sense of the fitness of the finest materials for the highest purpose. When therefore they came to depict the scenes of the Gospels in embroidery, gold thread was the material chosen for the holy figures themselves. Only the flesh parts and hair were worked in silk, and this arrangement remained in force virtually during the whole history of embroidery in the Orthodox church.

Since embroidery is by definition worked on a ground material already existing, the type and colour of this material and its relationship to the embroidery must be considered. Many western embroideries covered the ground entirely, completely transforming a material in itself commonplace. The normal Byzantine practice was to use a dark red or dark blue silk, both shades which were allied to the imperial purple, and treat this as a foil for the gold figures. They did on occasion cover all the background with gold as well, but the principle that the figures themselves

[65] A. Hadjimichaeli, Τα Χρυσοκλαβαρικὰ – συρματέϊνα – συρμακέσικα κεντήματα, in Mélanges Merlier, Vol II, pp. 447ff., Institut Français d'Athènes, 1956.

must be gold always remained. After the Byzantine period background colours tended to lighten, although red and blue remained the most popular. The Moldavians occasionally used a bright sky blue which was a startling departure from the sober Byzantine colours. During the latter part of the seventeenth century the contrast between colour and gold was sometimes abandoned in favour of an entirely golden image, and many late seventeenth and eighteenth century epitaphioi are worked on backgrounds of gold-coloured silk. Velvet was apparently not used at all as a ground material before the seventeenth century. Backgrounds that have been worked all over in coloured silk *embroidery* are all restorations, done because the original silk material had rotted.

Some understanding of the techniques of gold embroidery is essential to this study, since a comparison of technical details is often at least as helpful in dating a given piece as consideration of the artistic aspect, so extremely conservative was the iconography of embroidery designers. Technical styles, of course, also changed very slowly, and dating by this method alone can seldom narrow the limits to less than half a century. Short of an actual date, however, or definite knowledge of the donor, this is in any case nearly impossible.

With a few exceptions, embroiderers of all countries and periods have usually considered it impracticable to use gold as a sewing thread in the sense of threading it into a needle and passing it in and out of a piece of material. The classic method of handling gold, technically described as laid and couched, is to lay lengths of gold thread flat on the ground material and attach them to it by stitches made with a silk thread, usually between one eighth and one quarter of an inch apart. This silk thread is known as the couching thread, and it will be obvious that stitches made with it, which are at right angles to the gold and usually attach two threads of gold at a time, will show on the surface. The silk, of course does not pass through the gold, but over it (fig. **g**). Gold worked in this way can be used as an outline, but is more often laid in close rows to cover a given area completely. When the limit of this area is reached the double gold thread is turned back on itself and couched into the next row. Eventually the ends of the gold threads are carried to the back of the ground material with the aid of a stiletto and a loop of thread.

This method presupposes that the work is done on a frame, since a taut surface is necessary if the gold is to lie flat, and the worker needs both hands free to manipulate gold and silk threads. A silk ground material, unless it is quite exceptionally heavy, needs a backing of linen to strengthen it for the strain of framing and the weight of the finished embroidery.

All church embroidery in gold, in the Middle Ages and since, and nearly all gold embroidery on uniforms and other forms of dress, has been carried out by this basic method, but certain adaptations are possible, and these provide the

Figure **g.** *Couched gold threads*

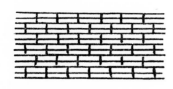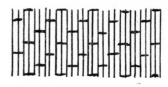

Figure **h.** *Surface couching (in section). Underside couching*

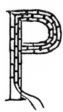

Figure **i.** *Lettering*

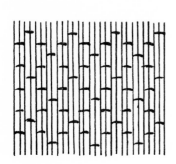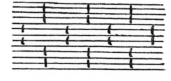

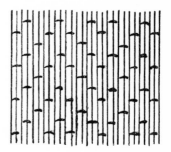

Figure **j.** *Some couching patterns*

Figures **g** *to* **j.** (*see page 66*).

hall-mark of place and period. Laid gold imposes its own restrictions, and the variations which can be made are not nearly as extensive as those offered by the different stitches in silk embroidery, but it also demands its own expertise and understanding from the worker, apart from the sheer technical skill and precision required, which are considerable. The Byzantines and their followers had their own methods of solving the problems, as did workers in other countries.

The first, simplest, and almost universal method of giving some variety to gold work is to make patterns with the couching stitches, which, since they can be seen clearly on the surface even when worked in gold-coloured silk, must in any case be placed with regularity. The most straightforward device is to alternate the stitches on each succeeding row of gold threads, which produces a simple basket pattern, and is the nearest thing to a flat gold surface that can be obtained. 41 More elaborate arrangements of the stitches result in various surface patterns on the gold. Western embroiderers had carried these patterns to a high degree of refinement at an early date and continued to use many variations during the late Middle Ages. The Byzantines were less adventurous in this respect and seldom departed from their favourite chevron, irresistibly reminiscent of herring-bone 100 tweed, throughout the fourteenth century. Later arrangements produced bricking, diamonds, zig-zags, and other patterns, a few of which are reproduced at fig. **j**. It is a mistake to regard these patterns as different *stitches*. In the strict technical sense gold embroidery knows no stitch but couching, and these are merely simple variations on the basic method.

Another, highly skilled version in use in the Middle Ages is known today as underside couching. In this a strong linen couching thread was drawn so tightly at every stitch that the gold thread was pulled through the ground material and appeared in a tiny loop on the underside, held there by the taut couching thread, which in this case was not seen on the surface of the finished work. Instead a pattern of tiny dents appeared where the gold entered the ground material, and the same designs could of course be made as in surface couching (fig. **h**).

This method was used in Sicily, and occasionally in France and Italy, but it was brought to its highest perfection in England during the late thirteenth and fourteenth centuries. It is in fact regarded as one of the distinguishing features of English work. I have not, on the other hand, found any trace of it in existing Byzantine or post-Byzantine embroidery, and have come to the conclusion that it was a technique unknown to Byzantine embroiderers. Post-Byzantine workers were so conservative in their methods that it seems highly unlikely that they would not have used it if the tradition had been handed on to them, and by the time their work became more experimental underside-couching had long fallen into disuse in the west.[66]

[66] The two roundels with Christ Pantocrator and the Virgin which decorate the mantle of Philip of Schwaben now at Speyer (*ca.*1200) are certainly very Byzantine in appearance, but because

Mere arrangement of the couching stitches will provide as many patterns as the imagination of the embroiderer can conceive, but it obviously has its limitations. Two problems which call for greater artistic understanding are the introduction of colour and the play of light on the gold itself. With these is bound up the use of different qualities and types of gold thread.

The Byzantines, as we have seen, liked their vestments embroidered in gold rather than colour, and relied chiefly on the deep contrast of the silk background to throw the gold into relief. Neither they nor their successors, at any rate until a much later date, used the combination of coloured silk against a gold background which was the west European solution to the problem in the fourteenth century.[67] When gold backgrounds were used, they relied on a change of direction in the gold threads or a change of pattern to differentiate between figures and background.

They did, however, introduce undertones of colour into the gold by using different qualities of gold thread, or silver thread, or coloured silk twisted with gold or silver. The designer of the Salonica epitaphios was a supreme master of of these subtle, barely realised changes in colour, and no other existing piece can quite match it. It is also the only existing epitaphios which is embroidered entirely in gold and silver with no visible background material.

Two kinds of metal thread were used in Byzantine work. The first was a very fine wire, either of a pale, soft, faintly green gold, or of silver with a bluish tinge. Thread which is described as gold, although sometimes pure gold in early centuries, is in fact nearly always silver gilt. Later the gold was often adulterated, and by the seventeenth century both gold and silver were harsher in tone and presented a cruder contrast to each other.

The second was a twisted thread consisting of a very fine flat strip of metal wound round a coloured silk core, for which the Greek name is *chryssónima*. This could be used tightly twisted, as it was in the west in the Middle Ages and still is today, so that the silk was entirely hidden, or deliberately less tightly wound so that the coloured core was allowed to show and so tint the gold. The twisted thread was so fine that it can only be distinguished under a magnifying glass, and the visible effect is simply a faint flush of colour which gives life and contrast to

they are underside couched I wonder if they could not have come from Sicily. This theory is born out by the fact that although Philip was married to a Byzantine princess, Irene, daughter of the Emperor Isaac II Angelus, she had previously been married to the eldest son of Tancred of Lecce, King of Sicily, who predeceased his father. According to Hampe (Das Hochmittelalter, 1953, p. 311) Philip ' came upon ' the widowed Irene in the Palace at Palermo, whence she could well have brought either the embroidery itself or a Sicilian embroiderer to her German court.

[67] This technique seems to have been used in Russia much earlier than in other Orthodox countries, possibly as a result of western influence.

the golden surface. Coloured silk was also occasionally twisted with a gold or silver wire thread, which naturally allowed rather more colour to show and produced a slightly textured effect. Byzantine workers usually, but not invariably, laid their gold over an underlay of soft cotton threads, and where the gold was coloured the underlay was sometimes coloured to match. None of it was left showing, however, and it can have had only the very faintest effect on the colour of the gold thread.

This colouring was used with such discretion in the Salonica epitaphios that the first impression is simply of a great richness of gold and silver, and only closer study brings a realisation of the colours used. The same methods became very popular in Rumania at the end of the fifteenth and beginning of the sixteenth centuries, and were used there with rather greater freedom. More coloured silk and less gold appeared in the twisted thread, so that the image presented was one of gold and colour, rather than gold suffused with colour. It must be realised of course that in all these embroideries the gold-and-silk thread was only used in certain places, and fairly large areas of plain gold occurred as well. As time wore on the twisted thread was used with less and less sublety, and by the middle of the sixteenth century sometimes created rather a harsh effect. The coloured silk was in many cases simply red, blue and green and was not in itself particularly pleasing. It was only when it was used as a discreet foil to the gold that it achieved its purpose of bringing life and warmth to the embroidery.

During the seventeenth century *chryssónima* was in general out of fashion in favour of a purely gold and silver effect which sought to imitate goldsmith's work, but the eighteenth century saw a revival of the style. The best workers of this period used it with care to introduce areas of coloured shading in a more naturalistic manner than had previously been attempted.

A highly sophisticated solution to the relationship of gold and colour was produced in western Europe during the fifteenth century. This, known as *or nué*, was basically nothing more than the use of coloured couching threads on the gold, but the working of the couching stitches in shading instead of in formal patterns, and the artistry which controlled the amount of gold left showing by the density of these stitches, transformed this apparently simple method into one of the most elaborate forms of gold embroidery. Its greatest surviving monument is the set of vestments made in the Low Countries for the Order of the Golden Fleece in the middle of the fifteenth century, and now in the Schatzkammer in Vienna. By this time, when the technique was established in western Europe, the Orthodox lands were already cut off by the Turkish advance, and *or nué* never penetrated to the east, just as coloured *chryssónima* never found acceptance in the west. Coloured couching threads are sometimes used in post-Byzantine embroidery to obtain small geometric patterns in colour, which is not the same as *or nué*.

With the exception of the beige used for flesh parts and the brown or white and blue used for hair, the Byzantines never used coloured silk to cover a surface, and so avoided the criticism, if criticism it is held to be, that they tried to emulate painting in a medium which should rely on its own technique for its effects. In this it may be that they were influenced by the impressionistic methods of their own mosaicists in handling colour and mass, although no embroidery, even the Salonica epitaphios, reached anything like the sophisticated levels of the mosaics in this direction. They did treat literally the linear style of Byzantine drawing, and coloured silks, usually in the same colours as the *chryssónima*, were used to emphasise the lines of the inner drawing of figures and features.

It has been explained that laid gold is normally turned back on itself at the edge of the area to be covered. Fourteenth and fifteenth century embroiderers regarded this area as the space between any two drawing lines. They turned their gold thread frequently and left all the inner drawing in reserve, filling the channels with lines of coloured silk in stem or split stitch. This gives the embroidery a characteristic appearance, leaving a tiny ridge of gold on each side of the drawing lines. Later generations grew lazy about turning their gold, which is a finicky and relatively time-taking operation, and sometimes carried it over the inner drawing, putting in the silk line over the gold threads.

34

By the seventeenth century coloured lines were often dispensed with, and as we have seen, all colour was unfashionable, perhaps because the decline in the proper use of *chryssónima* had given designers a dislike of the technique. Instead a pair of gold threads would be carried over several drawing lines and the couching stitches placed on the lines themselves, so that the drawing was in fact executed in couching. An alternative method was to couch the gold on each side of a string underlay which outlined the drawing, creating a thick line of raised gold down the folds of garments. This all-gold style also relied heavily on couching patterns. At its best it reached extremely high technical standards but its effect was a little soulless compared to earlier work.

45

All that glitters may not be gold, but gold must glitter, especially when its purpose is the glorification of a rite. The embroiderer must bear this in mind, and a true understanding of working in gold threads involves consideration of the play of light on the gold at different angles. This question also has had varying solutions at different periods. English medieval embroiderers couched their gold in general vertically, that is in line with the warp of the ground material. One of their most brilliant effects was to produce elaborate patterns in gold on gold by using horizontal threads in contrast. They seldom departed from these two directions, but a changing play of light was further encouraged by the fall of the circular vestments, the bell chasuble and the cope, on which their best work was done. In modern times great attention is paid to variations in light on a curve.

Byzantine workers do not seem to have considered couching gold to follow a curved outline. Even haloes were worked from side to side, and post-Byzantine embroiderers did not treat their haloes as a circle until late in the seventeenth century. Nor was their embroidery done on garments which helped the play of light by their own cut and movement. Byzantine craftsmen, however, seem to have been acutely conscious of the subtleties required to release the latent fire in any golden surface. Mosaicists curved their plaster beds and laid their tesserae at minutely different angles. Embroiderers altered, if only by a few degrees, the direction of their laid threads in adjacent areas to achieve the same effect.   58, 103

This purpose is not always apparent to the present day observer, who sees the embroidery laid flat in a show case under an even light. The gold is in greater or lesser degree tarnished, and if the different angles of its laying are observed at all, they appear haphazard, even due to carelessness, although in fact the carelessness, or rather lack of care, arose when attention was no longer paid to these directional niceties. Once I was privileged, by accident I must admit, rather than from choice, to see an epitaphios by the light of a hurricane lamp. In this warm, smoky light, which moved across the surface as I held it, trying to see each part of the veil, the faded gold sprang suddenly to life and the figures shone forth as they must once have done in the flickering candlelight for which the work was designed, pointing the lesson of the carefully laid and constantly changing gold surface.

A point should be noted here about the treatment of lettering, which we have seen played a much greater part in Byzantine embroidery than it did in the west. The Byzantines always couched their gold thread across the *width* of the stroke, whereas in the west the gold was laid to follow the outline of the letter (fig. **i**). The latter method was used on the Genoa altar cloth, and for this reason it seems likely that the inscriptions, which were all written in Latin, were actually worked by a Latin embroiderer.

Until at any rate the middle of the sixteenth century, virtually only two types of metal thread had been used, the traditional wire and *chryssónima*. During the seventeenth century gold-embroidered Turkish dress became increasingly popular in all the countries under Turkish rule. Although a fine wire thread was often used for this type of embroidery, its workers not unnaturally needed to obtain their effect by rather quicker methods, and this resulted in the production of a two-ply twisted gold and silver thread, like a miniature rope, and a three-ply   114
plait, both of which could be couched in the same way as the single threads. Both were used in church embroideries during the seventeenth and eighteenth centuries. At about the same time gold bullion was also introduced. This is a coil of wire with a hollow centre which can be cut off in the required lengths and   55
sewn down like a bead. It was known by its Turkish name of *tir-tir*, and usually used in church embroidery in the subsidiary pattern.

In Byzantine times and for at least a century or more after, the embroideries

71

were always flat in appearance, even if an underlay of cotton threads had been used below the gold. This also changed during the seventeenth century, whether due to the example of Turkish embroidery or the infiltration of baroque influence from the west, and a certain amount of padding, of felt or paper or the like, was used under the gold to produce a raised effect.

This padding was carried to greater lengths in Russia, especially during the seventeenth century. Another method common in Russian embroidery of this period but never found in Greece and the Balkans was the use of applied pieces of material, usually a coloured brocade with a small gold patern, to fill parts of the design. The brocade took the place of the traditional couching patterns, and was naturally much quicker to work than laid gold. This and the effect of relief produced by padding made the Russian embroideries of this period altogether bolder and less restrained in style than those which remained closer to the Byzantine tradition.

So far we have considered only the handling of gold thread, which indeed made up almost the whole of these embroideries. The Byzantines used silk embroidery only for flesh and hair. These were worked in split stitch, with eyes and other features drawn in fine lines of black or brown silk. This in fact was the normal method everywhere during the later Middle Ages. Some early English and south German embroiderers included the flesh in the gold embroidery, but this practice seems to have ceased by the middle of the thirteenth century, and there is no existing Byzantine example.

The silk stitchery in the best examples followed the natural contours of the flesh, but there seems to have been very little attempt at shading, although the almost complete lack of variation in the flesh colours may to some extent be due to fading. Faces in later years, when the workers grew careless, were often worked in a uniformly vertical direction which removed all character from the features. Characterisation in faces is not as difficult for the competent embroiderer as the layman might suppose, and lack of artistry in this respect is invariably a sign of decadence. Late post-Byzantine pieces sometimes have painted and applied silk, or even enamel plaques, substituted for embroidery in the flesh parts. The result is a sadly sentimental caricature of the early tradition.

Hair was always treated in formal lines of split stitch following the accepted
100 pattern of waves or curls for the person represented. Alternate lines of two browns were usual, or of white and blue for white hair. In this, and in the treatment of flesh, there is a very marked resemblance between medieval English and Byzantine embroidery, although the Byzantines did not follow their split stitch contours quite as elaborately as the English workers, whose spiral cheeks remain famous and unique.

This method of treating flesh and hair and the division between silk for these and gold for the rest of the work remained until very late in post-Byzantine times.

At the end of the seventeenth century the Constantinopolitan embroideress Despoineta turned deliberately to Italy for inspiration, and her manner of working flesh parts was certainly influenced by Italian embroidery. It involved the use of a much softer floss silk and the stitch technically known as long-and-short instead of the medieval split stitch. This, when finely worked, produces a flat surface hardly distinguishable as stitchery at all, and when allied to careful shading has the effect of painting. The style remained in use throughout the eighteenth century, as did the introduction of coloured silk details in decoration.

The embroideries of Christopher Žefarović, which departed so far from tradition as to use coloured silk for the figures and confine the gold to the decoration, have already been mentioned, but as we have seen the use of the western technique may have been the natural result of giving the work to a western (Viennese) workroom.

Pearls were used lavishly by many medieval and Renaissance embroiderers, and not least by the Byzantines and their successors. Illustrations and contemporary descriptions of Byzantine court dress suggest rich decorations of pearls and precious or semi-precious stones. We are told that the jewels on the costume of the Emperor Manuel Comnenus resembled a ' meadow strewn with flowers ',[68] but pearls especially seem to have been used for religious embroideries in Byzantine times and since.

The description in the Vatican inventory of 1295 of the Lyons curtain[69] speaks of ' a representation of Our Saviour in gold, the folds of whose robes are picked out with pearls ', and again, ' in the border of the said cloth there are Greek and Latin letters and pearls throughout the border of the said cloth; there are also pearls throughout the haloes of the Saints and the persons represented and throughout the folds of their robes '. From existing embroideries with the pearls still intact, such as the epigonation of the Dormition[70] at Putna and the saccos of the Metropolitan Photius in Moscow, it would seem that pearls were not handled   7, 8
with great imagination but traditionally used for outlining haloes or even whole figures. In fact when used in quantity they seem to obscure the embroidery and were obviously intended to produce a sumptuous appearance from a distance, when the finer points would in any case be lost. An enormous quantity of the pearls that once decorated medieval embroideries has now disappeared, through robbery or accident. Byzantine embroideries are no exception, and many a halo that is now plain must once have had its pearly border. The same fate has overtaken any precious stones that were used on the older pieces, although some eighteenth century work has still retained stones and glass beads.

[68] J. Ebersolt, Les arts somptuaires de Byzance, 1923, p. 86.
[69] Quoted in L. de Farcy, La Broderie de l'XIième siècle jusqu'à nos jours, 1895, p. 35.
[70] Millet, Broderies, pl. CXXXII.

CHAPTER NINE

EMBROIDERY AND HISTORY

BYZANTIUM AND SERBIA

The course of history naturally had its effect on the production of these embroideries. As a plant must depend on favourable soil and nourishment for healthy growth, so the sumptuary arts depended on an atmosphere of opulence and wealthy patronage in which to thrive. This they found *par excellence* in Constantinople. Even though it has been argued that embroidery was in itself an economy measure, this was strictly relative. No one who has read Steven Runciman's moving account of the city before the Turkish conquest[71] can doubt that the great days of its magnificence had gone; no one equally can doubt that if its splendours were quietly fading and its population dwindling this was merely by comparison with its earlier glories, which had so overwhelmed the first Crusaders. The Constantinople of the Palaeologi was still the imperial city, the centre of learning and of artistic inspiration, above all the hub of a society where piety went hand in hand with a love of luxury and display, and men sought insurance for the welfare of their souls in eternity by lavish gifts to churches here on earth.

Outside the capital embroidery flourished in similar conditions, and these were chiefly provided in the atmosphere of a ruling court. It is impossible to speak of stability in connection with South-Eastern Europe at this period. Both Byzantium and the Balkan countries lived in a more or less perpetual state of war, against each other and against the ever-present, ever-growing aggression of the Turks. The essential condition was rather a springing self-confidence, the *élan* which caused a ruler, however precariously balanced his throne, to build and endow churches and to import from Constantinople the luxurious appurtenances which would lay the foundations for his own craft workshops. At the same time a court became the centre of a ruling society which in its turn provided patronage

---

[71] S. Runciman. The Fall of Constantinople 1453. 1965, pp. 9-11.

for the products of these workrooms.[72] When invasion, defeat, and taxation imposed by a conqueror crushed a ruling class, the minor arts were among the first casualties.

Constantinople then was the foremost centre. It was presumably here that the pair of veils at Halberstadt, the gift of an Alexius Palaeologus to an unknown church, was made. They probably date from the last years of the twelfth century. A much restored altar cloth in the Treasury at St. Mark's in Venice which is decorated with two embroidered angels, the gift of a Constantine Angelus, may belong to the same period.[73] These two pieces are the only surviving examples from before the Frankish conquest of the city.

85, 86

An inventory at Patmos[74] dating from about 1201 lists veils, altar coverings, priestly vestments, stoles, etc. among the treasures of the monastery, most of which seem to have been made of brightly coloured silks. Others are said to have been woven with gold, and some may have been gold embroidery. A vestment which was said to have belonged to the Patriarch was described as being decorated with figures. None of these, however, appear to have survived.

The barons of the Fourth Crusade, who sacked Constantinople in 1204 and established themselves there with the title of emperor, ruled it until 1261. This political disaster to the Byzantine state seems in fact to have made little real impact in the world of the arts, but we simply do not know how it affected the various craft workshops in the city. One would suppose that the Frankish emperors, striving ineffectually to fill the great role which they nominally held, would have used to the full the means they had to hand for producing a display of magnificence, but if they obliged Greek embroiderers to work for them, we have no record of it, unless perhaps the Grandson frontal[75] can be regarded as a product of this period.

---

[72] In the Balkan countries of course gold embroidery was a prime luxury. The question of its taking second place to a leading silk industry did not arise, except in so far as silks were imported.

[73] It has been suggested that this cloth was the one promised to Venice by the Despot Michael I of Epirus in his Treaty with the Venetians of 1210, and that the Constantine of the inscription is Michael's son, who is mentioned in the Treaty. (M. Theocaris, Sur le Sébastocrator Constantin Commène Ange et l'endyté du Musée de St. Marc à Venise, in BZ Vol. 56, No. 2, Dec. 1963).

This Treaty, however, is the only mention of Constantine. He never succeeeded his father and is assumed to have died in childhood. It seems therefore extremely unlikely that his name would have figured as the only donor, if this were indeed the cloth of Michael's Treaty. Another suggestion is that Constantine was the brother of the Emperors Isaac II and Alexius III Angelus (V. Laurent, Revue des études byzantines XVIII 1960, p. 208-213).

[74] C. Diehl, Le trésor de la bibliothèque de Patmos, BZ, I, 1892, p. 488.

[75] This famous piece in the Historisches Museum in Berne was given to Lausanne cathedral by an unknown member of the Grandson family. It is evidently of Greek workmanship although, like the Genoa frontal, it was obviously made for a western church, and is generally assumed to have been brought back from the Crusades. Another suggestion is that it is the work of Greeks in exile.

Meanwhile three rival branches of the deposed imperial family had established themselves in Nicaea, Trebizond and Epirus, where they each set up a court in the Byzantine style. Nicaea, which eventually provided the next established dynasty, was probably the leader of the three, but each capital-in-exile must to some extent have supported the luxury crafts. Joannina in Epirus received and sheltered a particularly large number of refugees from Constantinople, and it is perfectly possible that artists were among them. A specific mention of vestments for the church in the Despotate of Epirus comes from the period when Constantinople was in Byzantine hands again. Theodora, wife of the Despot Michael II, who had a reputation for saintliness, founded a convent in Arta where she herself retired after Michael's death in 1271. We are told that she endowed the church with vestments,[76] but we do not know what they were like, or whether they were of local workmanship. Theodora travelled a good deal in her attempts to compose her husband's differences with Michael VIII Palaeologus, and had plenty of opportunity for ordering vestments for her church in Salonica or Constantinople.

Some years earlier, in the spring of 1461, Michael VIII himself, at that moment crowned emperor but still exiled in Nicaea, enlisted the help of the Genoese in his efforts to recapture Constantinople. The treaty signed at Nymphaion in Asia Minor provided for Genoese naval intervention in return for considerable trading rights when the city should be taken, and as a further gesture Michael promised three altar cloths to the City and Cathedral of Genoa. One of these still exists.[77] The cross-in-circle motif which decorates the background, the ornament of the border and much of the technique point to a Byzantine workroom, but it is obvious that Michael went out of his way to please his western allies. This is clear from the choice of western saints (the Cathedral at Genoa is dedicated to St. Lawrence and the scenes illustrated include St. Lawrence and two martyrs associated with him, St. Sixtus and St. Hippolytus), and the Latin inscriptions, but the long rectangular form of the cloth and the arrangement of the scenes in a double frieze are not typical of embroideries made for use in Byzantine churches. It is fairly certain, from the technique, that the inscriptions were not only written but also embroidered by a Latin. If Michael had the commission executed in Constantinople when he entered the city four months after the treaty, rather than in Nicaea, it argues that he found a gold embroidery workroom functioning when he arrived.

Michael VIII seems to have favoured embroidered vestments when imperial gifts were called for. One of the periodic discussions between Greeks and Latins on the question of reuniting the two churches took place at the Council of Lyons in 1274. On this occasion Michael's ambassadors presented an altar cloth to

[76] D. M. Nichol, The Despotate of Epiros, 1957, p. 201.
[77] In the Palazzo Bianco in Genoa. It is possible that only one of the three was ever sent.

76

Pope Gregory X, which appears to have been a long curtain, described in the west as *dorsale*. It evidently had the Trinity at the top, with a bust of the Virgin with saints in the middle, and below that again St. Peter, to whom Gregory is leading Michael. Round the whole was a border of vines enclosing scenes from the lives of the Apostles. All the embroidery was richly decorated with pearls.[78] This description seems to suggest that later Moldavian curtains with similar borders at Putna and Slatina were based on a Byzantine model.

The great period for Byzantine embroidery was the fourteenth and first half of the fifteenth centuries, when artistic activity in Constantinople reached its final brilliant climax in spite of the slow decay which was gradually overtaking the city. The Byzantines, inconveniently for the historian, were not as a rule given to dating their embroideries, so that we can only estimate the dates of two magnicient pieces from this period, the saccos in the Treasury of St. Peter's in Rome, and the Salonica epitaphios, both of which are ascribed to the fourteenth century· Two very fine Byzantine sacci connected with the Metropolitan Photius of Moscow (1408-32) have also survived.

1-6
95
7-14

The splendour of these pieces indicates that there must have been many more of their kind, but in fact surviving Byzantine examples from the fourteenth century are rare. In addition to the sacci we can count three or four epitaphioi, the earliest of them St. Clement of Ochrid, dating from the last years of the thirteenth century, and a handful of stoles, epigonatia and aëres.

93

At this period Salonica was a thriving, immensely wealthy city acting as the main trading entrepôt for the whole of Thessaly, Macedonia, Thrace and Serbia. All the nationalities of the Near East and the Mediterranean gathered at her trade fairs, where the merchandise ranged from cattle to caviare and from honey to the finest silks. A large share of the city's wealth was concentrated in the hands of the church, which celebrated the feast of the city's patron, Saint Demetrius, with processions of unrivalled grandeur.[79] The famous epitaphios, finest of all the surviving embroideries, was presumably used for this occasion, when all the churches were magnificently decorated, but we do not know if it was made in the city or in Constantinople. Certainly Salonica must be regarded as a likely centre for embroidery on this scale.

One other town must be considered as a possible home of the minor arts. This was Mistra in the Peloponnese, which was returned to Byzantine hands after the defeat of the Franks and the capture of their leaders at the battle of Pelagonia in 1259. This dramatic fortress became the seat of the Greek Despots of the Morea, and during the fourteenth century earned its place in artistic history with

---

[78] L. de Farcy, La broderie de l'XIme siècle jusqu'à nos jours, p. 35.
[79] O. Tafrali, Thessalonique au quatorzième siècle, 1912, pp. 118ff., 138ff.

a series of tiny, perfect churches, decorated with frescoes which reveal late Byzantine art in its finest moment.

We have one embroidery from the beginning of the fifteenth century which may be connected with the Morea through its donor, the Nicholas Eudaimono-ioannes epitaphios. A member of a famous Peloponnesian family, archons of Monemvasia since before the Frankish conquest, Nicholas may be presumed to have presented his epitaphios either to a church in his home town or to one in Mistra. Whether he commissioned it locally or not is another matter, and one more question to which there is no answer.

It was during the fourteenth century that church embroidery spread to the Balkans. As the nomad tribes which had moved southwards into the peninsuala during the sixth to the eighth centuries gradually settled, and eventually united in different areas under leaders strong enough to form separate kingdoms, the conditions necessary for the well-being of artistic life were established in one nascent state and then another.

The earliest to achieve this degree of civilisation was the kingdom of Bulgaria, which ruled a large part of the Balkans during the tenth century until their defeat by the Emperor Basil II (the Bulgar-slayer) in 1018. It was Bulgaria which received the disciples of St. Cyril when they were driven from Moravia at the end of the ninth century, and established them at Ochrid, and it was the work of these early missionaries which won the Balkan peninsula for the Orthodox church and ensured that Balkan civilisation would be modelled on Byzantium, and that the Balkan churches, and art in the service of these churches, would find their inspiration and the mainspring of their life in Byzantine models.

We have, however, no embroidery from the first Bulgarian kingdom, and indeed at this early period none from Byzantium either. Even when in 1186 the house of Asen won eastern Macedonia back from the Byzantines, and established a second Bulgarian kingdom based on Trnovo, which remained powerful throughout the thirteenth and fourteenth centuries, there is no surviving embroidery which can be called Bulgarian.

Meanwhile Serbia had achieved the status of an independent kingdom under Stephen Nemanya in the second half of the twelfth century. Stephen and his sons imported from Constantinople the icons which were to lay the foundations of Serbian graphic art in the following two centuries. During the thirteenth century, the influence of Byzantine art, transmitted through Salonica and Ochrid, was very strong in Macedonia and Serbia, although the extreme sophistication and idealised elegance of Constantinopolitan art at this period was transformed by the Serb icon and fresco painters into an extremely personal expression of feeling more concerned with human emotions and reactions, even with the recording of human portraits, than the aloof mysticism which had, at any rate hitherto, been the preoccupation of Byzantium. By the end of the century, Serb fresco painting was well-established in its own paths, and while artists continued to draw their inspiration from Byzantium, the national character of their work was unmistakeable.

The same cannot be said of embroidery, which appears to have remained very true to the Byzantine style. It is only from the turn of the thirteenth century that the earliest of the embroideries connected with Serbia and Macedonia appear.

The first of them are two epitaphioi, neither of which are dated, but which from their donors can be regarded as roughly contemporary. They are incidentally the earliest of all the known epitaphioi, and both of course are the liturgical type.

One, which has already been mentioned, is presumably Constantinopolitan 93 work, the gift of the Emperor Andronicus II Palaeologus, who reigned from 1282 to 1328, to the church of St. Clement at Ochrid, a town which during these centuries suffered a confused history between the Bulgars, the Byzantines, the Greek Despotate of Epirus and the Serbs. It had been secured, with other Macedonian fortresses, for Michael VIII Palaeologus against his rival the Despot of Epirus, in 1259, the year that he became emperor. Andronicus, Michael's son, was a pious man interested in church affairs, who had no use for his father's efforts to unite the churches for political reasons. Andronicus gave no embroideries to the west, still less does his epitaphios show any signs of western design or technique. Many embroideries appear to have been given to St. Clement at the time of its foundation in 1295. They are even mentioned, among other things, in the inscription over the church door. Some are listed and illustrated by Kondakov,[80] but unfortunately most of these, including the epitaphios, are now missing. It is impossible to tell whether they were made in Ochrid itself, or brought from Constantinople or Salonica. Andronicus evidently continued to take an interest in the archbishopric throughout his reign, since he later presented the Metropolitan Gregory with a monastery in Constantinople which was administered on behalf of the Archbishop by a monk from Ochrid.

Serbia meanwhile was ruled by Stephen Uroš II Milutin, whose reign from 1282 to 1321 exactly paralleled that of Andronicus. In fact he scandalised the church in his later years by taking as his fourth wife Andronicus's five-year-old daughter, but even if his matrimonial affairs left something to be desired, he was a great patron of the arts in Serbia. He is assumed to be the donor of an epitaphios 94 signed Milutin Ureš, which is thus of approximately the same date as St. Clement, the oldest of the existing Serb embroideries.

If St. Clement can be regarded as representing the Constantinopolitan style of the period, it can be seen that Serb embroideries stayed very close to their

[80] N. P. Kondakov, Makedoniya, 1909, pp. 272-274. The podea with the Presentation of the Virgin, illustrated at fig. 187, is now in the National Museum, at Ochrid. It is probably of later date than the foundation of the church.

models. This becomes even more obvious with the much more elaborate epitaphios of Archbishop John of Skopje at Chilandari,[81] dating from the middle years of the fourteenth century, which is even closer to the Salonica epitaphios than to St. Clement. This has a wide border with Feasts in rectangular compartments, and a frieze representing the Eucharist at the bottom.

Another epitaphios at the same monastery presents some difficulties with regard to the date.[82] A long dedicatory inscription in Slavonic states that it is offered by ' the sinner John . . . to the honour and glory of the Archistrategos Michael and our beloved Father Gabriel, hermit '. A curt addition to the main inscription reads, ' Hand of the sinner Syropoulos '. Mirković connects this veil with the monastery of Lesnovo, which was dedicated to the ' Great Voivod of the Heavenly Troops, the supreme Commander Michael, and the grave of the Father Gabriel ', and was founded by the Despot John Oliver in 1341; he regards Syropoulos as the embroiderer. In view of the wording of the dedication the attribution seems conclusive.

Millet, however, thinks that ' John ' and ' Syropoulos ' were the same person, and suggests that the epitaphios was presented to Chilandari by an official of the Patriarchate of that name in the 1390's.

On the other hand some points of the iconography and the apparent technical style could indicate a much later date. (Obviously, I have not seen this epitaphios, and photographs are notoriously misleading. It is possible that examination of the technique on the piece itself would suggest that it is earlier than appears from the illustration.) This is an early (perhaps the earliest) example of the Lamentation on an epitaphios. The Virgin and St. John are mourning behind the bier, and their formal attitudes (even the Mother of God is not touching the Body of her Son) suggest an early date. Angels above the bier and cherubim and thrones below may be compared to John of Skopje and Salonica, both of which date to the middle of the fourteenth century. At the same time three mourning women are included, which does not otherwise occur in embroidered epitaphioi until the end of the fifteenth century, and the Cross is shown behind the bier, which is not usual until the sixteenth. The representation of the Four Evangelists standing full length among the figures of the main scene has no parallel. Whether the epitaphios was the gift of John Oliver at or shortly after the foundation of the monastery, or whether it was given at some time during the fifteenth century (by the middle of the sixteenth Lesnovo was in ruins), this piece was in some respects ahead of its period.

[81] Millet, Broderies, p. 95ff. pls. CXXXIII, CCV-CCVII .

[82] Millet, Broderies, p. 102ff., pl. CLXXXVI; Mirković, Crkveni Umetnički Vez, p. 18, pl. VI; Stojanović, Umetnički Vez, No. 15.

From the end of the century we have the epitaphios of Euphemia, whose history has already been mentioned, and her curtain at Chilandari, which alone could stand as a monument to the ability of Serb embroiderers at this period. These pieces must have been made in central Serbia, after the battle of Kossovo. The epitaphios was later taken to Moldavia and is now at Putna. It is possible to trace a rather tenuous development, particularly in the border and background ornament, from St. Clement through Milutin Ureš to Euphemia, and thence to the Moldavian embroideries in the following century.

The great days of Serbian embroidery were confined almost exactly to the fourteenth century. This was also the period of Serbia's greatest political power, which attained its climax under Stephen Dušan (1336-55). By the last years of the century the Turks had overrun the whole of Byzantium's Asiatic possessions with the exception of Trebizond, and Constantinople itself, and were pushing relentlessly forward into Europe. The Serbs suffered two crushing defeats, at the Maritsa in 1371 and at Kossovo in 1389, where Lazar, the last of the independent Serb princes, was killed. His son Stephen Lazarević succeeded him with the title of Despot and as a vassal of the Sultan.

Even then Serbia's artistic life was not entirely crushed. Some churches were still built while the court remained and other artists were still working. The Despotate, however, was increasingly taxed and harried by the Turks, and in 1459 was completely overrun.

The middle years of the fifteenth century saw the end of every centre of Byzantine civilisation. Constantinople itself fell in 1453, Salonica passed finally into Turkish hands in 1430, and by the early 1460's Epirus, Mistra and Trebizond were all extinguished. This complete annihilation removed what, as we have seen, had been the first condition of professional church embroidery, the patronage of a wealthy ruling class. The Turks who captured Constantinople were proud of their fantastic prize, perhaps even overawed by it, and immediately set themselves to restore its splendours for their own benefit. They took over its historic silk weaving industry, and were soon producing silks in their own style that were to become as famous in their time as their Byzantine predecessors had been in the past. Equally they seem to have made use of the skill of the gold embroiderers, for Turkish gold-embroidered costume was later to become the fashionable dress of all the Balkan area. But this was a secular magnificence.[83] Although Christians were given a certain measure of freedom to worship, they can have had little occasion or encouragement in the early years after the conquest for the creation of luxury articles for the churches they were allowed to keep.

In the Balkans the Turkish conquest gradually reduced all society to the peasant level. The influence of the landowners and small nobility was slowly

[83] S. Runciman, The Fall of Constantinople 1453, 1965, p. 189.

undermined by the increasingly heavy taxation which eventually crushed them. Any artistic activity which survived was driven into the monasteries, where patriotism and the desperate need to cling to the faith excluded every draught which could have brought a breath of change or outside influence. This was the foundation of the extreme conservatism which was to kill church embroidery in the centuries to come.

THE RUMANIAN PRINCIPALITIES

While the Turks were pressing harder and harder in the south east and gradually establishing themselves as masters of the whole of that area, north of the Danube two new principalities were emerging from tribal conditions and carving for themselves the status of independent kingdoms. In the twelfth and thirteenth centuries the area now known as Rumania had been inhabited by small groups of tribes, most of whom owed allegiance to the King of Hungary. From the beginning of the fourteenth century the southern part of the country, Wallachia, found itself strong enough to throw off Hungarian suzerainty under an independent prince, and fifty years later Moldavia in the north followed suit.

The new principality of Moldavia, with its capital first at Baia and later at Suceava, lay on what was at this period one of the great European trade routes, connecting Prussia and Poland with south-eastern Europe and with Venetian and Genoese trading ports on the Black Sea. By the fifteenth century Moldavia was sufficiently organised to play an active part in this trade, and from the time of the Voivod Alexander the Good (1400-1432) it formed the basis of her prosperity.

Long before the establishment of the two principalities, disciples of St. Clement of Ochrid had brought Orthodox Christianity and the Slavonic language and alphabet to Rumania. Although his country was already committed to the Orthodox faith, Alexander the Good in the early part of his reign was eager for political reasons to remain on good terms with the Roman church. At this period he owed allegiance to King Ladislas of Poland, and his second wife, Ryngala, was a Lithuanian and a Catholic. At the time of his accession the Moldavian church was also at odds with Constantinople over the election of a metropolitan. From the 1420's all this was changed. Alexander divorced Ryngala and married a third wife, Marina, whose influence for Orthodoxy was considerable. Ecclesiastical differences with Constantinople were resolved, and in 1424 John VIII Palaeologus, on a journey through Moldavia, made presents to the monastery of Neamţ and granted autonomy to the Moldavian church. From this time onwards Orthodox influence was secure, and Byzantium provided the style, iconography and technical methods, as well as the aesthetic inspiration for the newly born Moldavian arts. Only architecture was affected by gothic currents from the west.

Four embroideries from the time of Alexander are known, but unfortunately two of them are now lost. These were a stole with Feasts which names the donors as Alexander and Marina,[84] and an epitaphios dated 1428.[85] Both have Greek inscriptions, and the epitaphios has an indiction number after the date, a practice more usual with Greek workers than in Moldavia.

Another stole with Feasts in linked circles from the monastery of Bistriţa also has Greek inscriptions, and from its style is amost certainly of Greek workmanship. It must be remembered that craftsmen of all kinds may have been among the many refugees from the Turks who found their way north at this period, and of course it is also possible that the stole itself was brought from Greece.

29

The epitaphios of 1428, which was the last in the purely liturgical style, was clearly based on a Byzantine type, if not actually Greek work, and was one of two which obviously served as models for the later Moldavian epitaphioi. (The other was the epitaphios of Euphemia and Eupraxia.) It had the border of lettering used as decoration which was to become such a feature of the Moldavian style, although this was not an innovation. Such a border had already appeared on the epitaphios of Cozia in Wallachia and the Greek Nicholas Eudaimonoioannes epitaphios. It was also the first known example to introduce the words from the Liturgy, ἄδοντα, βοῶντα, κεκραγότα, λέγοντα in the arcs surrounding the Evangelists, which was another characteristic of the later Moldavian epitaphioi.[86]

97

101, 99

Both these points were taken up in the fourth embroidery from Alexander's period, the epitaphios given to Neamţ by the Abbot Siluan in 1437, which was clearly strongly influenced by certain Byzantine features, notably in the symbols of the Evangelists and the style of the angels. This, however, was the first of the Moldavian epitaphioi to introduce the Lamentation, and the first to place the Virgin at Christ's head instead of behind the bier.

102

The great age of Moldavian embroidery was to come in the second half of the fifteenth century with the reign of Stephen the Great, from 1457 to 1505. Stephen's long reign marked the height of Moldavian prosperity, in spite of the fact that he had to battle constantly against the Turks, now firmly established in the Balkans and eager to extend their conquests north of the Danube, as well as against the Hungarians and Poles, either of whom would have liked to annex the prosperous small state which had grown up on their borders. Stephen, as his suffix implies, was more than a good general. He was also a great statesman and an efficient economic administrator. If he was cruel and ruthless by modern

---

[84] Formerly in the Alexander Nevskij Museum in Leningrad. Millet, Broderies, p. 6, pl. VIII.

[85] Formerly in the monastery of Żółkiew in Poland. Illustrated in Revue roumaine d'histoire de l'art, 1, 1964, p. 65.

[86] Turdeanu has pointed out (Les épitaphes moldaves, p. 201) that the symbols of the Evangelists in the corners are found in Byzantine and Moldavian epitaphioi, but not in Serbian examples.

standards he was also a deeply religious man, whose piety took the form of building and endowing monasteries, some intended as seats of learning and artistic endeavour, others for purely practical purposes such as the care of soldiers wounded in his wars against the Turks. More than twenty built during his reign still exist.

Under his generous patronage the arts flourished. In architecture in particular, and in fresco painting and illumination, a marked Moldavian style developed from the Byzantine models which still provided the starting point. Stephen's earliest and most important foundation was the monastery of Putna, dedicated in 1469. Legend has it that Stephen, acting on the instructions of a hermit who was his spiritual mentor, established the site of the church by shooting an arrow into the air and building where it fell. The monastery was famous for its illuminated manuscripts. In addition, so many embroideries are connected with it, and are still preserved there, that it can safely be assumed that the main embroidery workshop of Stephen's reign was there as well. Indeed it is the only monastery of which this can be said with any degree of certainty, and certainly the only one which developed anything resembling a recognisable style of its own. It is also thought that there was a workroom in Stephen's capital at Suceava, and it is possible that embroideries were made at other monasteries.

The earliest embroidery at Putna is a stole with saints in arcades given by Stephen in 1469, but it is generally thought that this could not have been made there. The first manuscript copied in the monastery is dated 1470 and it seems unlikely that any of the arts were practised there earlier. Thereafter there is a succession of arcaded stoles, some of which are thought to be of Byzantine origin, or at least the work of Greek refugee artists, while others are regarded as copies made on the spot.[87] This theory is based on a comparison between the general appearance of proficiency of some of the stoles, combined with their Greek inscriptions, and the less able workmanship and Slavonic inscriptions of others. All these stoles have bands of ornament between the sections, but the tendency towards less ornament and even plainer presentation is very noticeable.

25, 36   Embroideries at Putna fall into two periods divided by a stole with Feasts signed by Stephen and his son Alexander, after the death of his second wife, Maria of Mangop. Although Maria's name is often mentioned in connection with
79   embroidery, this seems to be largely because her tomb cover, which is a beautiful work and one of the earliest of the great embroideries from Putna, has earned her a place in posterity. In fact she died in December 1477 and her reign in Moldavia was very short, but it is quite possible that her Byzantine upbringing led her to encourage the embroidery workrooms of her new home, and it is also possible, as

[87] See O Tafrali, Le Monastère de Putna, p. 56ff. for descriptions and illustrations of the compared stoles, also G. Millet, op cit. for illustrations, and E. Turdeanu, Les étoles, pp. 21ff. for a discussion of the whole question.

we have seen, that she brought embroiderers with her from her father's court at Mangop.

Apart from these two pieces from the period when Stephen was a widower, the finest of the Putna embroideries date from the last part of his reign and from the reign of his son, Bogdan the Blind, in the early years of the sixteenth century. It is true that the monastery was badly damaged by a fire in 1484, and we do not know how many earlier pieces may have been lost then. Stephen was married for a third time in 1480 to another Maria, Maria Voichiţa, a daughter of Radu the Handsome, Voivod of Wallachia, and most of the embroideries signed Stephen and Maria in fact refer to her and not to Maria of Mangop. Her portrait is embroidered with Stephen's on the large veil of the Crucifixion at Putna.[88]

It is not known how the epitaphios of Euphemia and Euphraxia reached Putna from Serbia, although it seems likely that it was taken to Moldavia by refugees from the Turks. It is of course nearly a hundred years older than the epitaphioi of Stephen's reign, but seems to have had a considerable influence on them. The background crowded with flower-stars was copied in the aër of the Abbot Anastasius and in three epitaphioi given by Stephen and Maria Voichiţa, one to Putna and the others to the now destroyed monastery of Moldoviţa, and to Dobrovaţ. **97** **105** **106**

Perhaps the finest of the Putna embroideries, and those which with the three epitaphioi show most clearly the establishment of a local style, are five large veils (two iconostasis curtains and three podeai or hangings for the sanctuary). The monastery church at Putna was dedicated to the Dormition of the Virgin, and two of them illustrate this subject, one from Stephen's reign, dated 1485, and the other from the time of Bogdan the Blind dated 1510[89] The others are an Ascension dated 1484, an Annunciation,[90] and the Crucifixion mentioned above dated 1500. **57** **56**

The big veil of the Dormition of 1510 recalls very closely in its vine-encircled border with scenes from the lives of the Apostles the Vatican description of the curtain given by Michael VIII to the Pope at the Council of Lyons (see p. 76 above) so that it seems possible that it was based on a Byzantine model, or at least on a description of this formula. It must itself have been the model for two curtains made for the monastery of Slatina in the middle of the sixteenth century. The broad sweeping arabesques of the foliage foreshadow the bolder style of sixteenth century ornament.

[88] A. R. P. R. Repertoriul, No. 95, fig. 212.

[89] A. R. P. R. Cultura Moldovenească, p. 274, fig. 5.

[90] A. R. P. R. Repertoriul, No. 111, fig. 236.

Most of the Byzantine embroideries which have survived are vestments which demanded a strict adherence to the liturgical subject (principally epitaphioi and stoles) but a few examples, notably the Vatican saccos, show that, given the opportunity, embroiderers and their designers could handle the most ambitious subjects in the truly monumental manner and with a sense of style and composition which raised embroidery to the level of the greater arts.

This tradition was preserved in the Putna veils. They not only look forward to the more detailed iconography which was adopted in the epitaphioi of the sixteenth and seventeenth centuries, but make in one giant stride the transition from the symbolic, purely liturgical representation to the realistic pictorial view of the fresco painters. These veils, and the two podeai at Grigoriou on Mount Athos, which may well have been gifts from Stephen and made in this same workroom,[91] are true embroidered pictures, complete with architectural settings for the action and living human beings to take part in it, as opposed the abstract expression of an ideal. Although the interest in realism and the human details of an enacted scene continued to occupy the designers of the sixteenth century, their work tended to fall back more and more on repetition and the inclusion of the ' required ' items, so that the greatest of the Putna embroideries stand unique.

The classic tradition established at Putna under Stephen the Great lasted throughout most of the following century. Embroidery flourished under Stephen's son Peter Rareş, who ruled from 1527-38 and again from 1541-46. He and his Serbian wife Helena presented an epitaphios to the monastery of Dionysiou on Mount Athos in 1545,[92] which is recognisably in the Putna style, although the background is surprisingly cluttered with decorative detail considering the general tendency to eliminate ornament in the middle of the sixteenth century. This is an epitaphios with the full iconography of the Lamentation, including Joseph and Nicodemus and as many as four women besides Mary Magdalene, as well as the Cross and Instruments of the Passion. The border of lettering, which has already lost some of the elegance of the great period, is supplemented by another which is a version of the linked circle and interlaced leaf type. This very persistent border pattern was still used in Rumania in the early years of the seventeenth century.

The ten years after Peter Rareş's death produced a series of stoles given to various monasteries by lesser Moldavian officials, which admirably illustrate the culmination of the stark undecorated style. The best of these, which can be linked to one workroom by the stylised flowers at the base, is a stole with the Great Feasts in the monastery of Dionysiou, the gift of the Hetman Dumitri.[93]

[91] Millet, Broderies, p. 85, pls. CLXX-I.
[92] Millet, Broderies, p. 107, pl. CXCI.
[93] Millet, Broderies, pl. XCV/4. See also pl. 43 below.

The last of the embroideries in the Putna tradition came when the Voivod Alexander Lăpușneanu founded the monastery of Slatina and presented to it an epitaphios dated 1556 which is strongly reminiscent of that of Peter Rareș, and   108 in 1561 the two curtains already mentioned which were undoubtedly inspired by   59, 65 the veil of 1510.

Towards the end of the century the Movila family, of which two brothers became Voivod, renovated the small monastery of Sucevița and built a new church. There is a number of embroideries connected with this foundation, many given by the wives of the two princes.[94] The most important of them are the tomb covers   81, 82 of the brothers themselves, Jeremiah and Simeon, which in spite of the classic Moldavian borders of lettering and linked circles, show a very marked change in atmosphere. Both brothers are dressed in a resplendent robe (possibly the same one) of Turkish silk. The care lavished by the embroiderer on reproducing the pattern of this brocade, which is the most striking part of both pieces, together with the flowers and cypress trees which decorate the background, herald the fascination which Turkish ornament was to have for embroidery designers in the following century. It may be remarked in passing that the band of floral decoration on the walls of the church at Sucevița was decidedly Turkish in character, and that a very similar pattern was used as a border in the embroideries made at Jassy during the 1630's.

Apart from the introduction of the new decorative style, the tomb cover of Simeon, the younger of the two brothers, appears to have been inspired by that of Maria of Mangop. Simeon is shown as on his deathbed, lying with closed eyes, with the traditional embroidered handkerchief between his folded hands. Jeremiah's, by contrast, is a forceful portrait of the living man, from which every trace of Byzantine stylisation of the figure has been removed.

Sucevița was the last monastic foundation to receive embroideries from the Moldavian princes. Apart from a brief flowering under Basil Lupu (the Wolf) at Jassy[95] in the 1630's, the days when the Moldavian court had the wealth and panache necessary for patronage of the arts on this scale were over. Although Stephen the Great had managed to hold off the Turks by force of arms, he had realised that this could not be done for long, and had advised his son to accept Turkish suzerainty. From the beginning of the sixteenth century therefore, the princes had paid tribute. Turkish demands gradually increased, the trade which had been the basis of Moldavian prosperity died out, economic conditions in general deteriorated, and the old noble families gradually lost their influence

[94] O. Tafrali, Sucevița.
[95] The capital had been transferred from Suceava to Jassy in 1564.

and standing. Professional embroidery was an expensive luxury which they could no longer afford.

83, 84   The embroideries at Jassy consist of tomb covers for Tudosca (Theodosia) the wife of Basil Lupu, and their son John, and five large veils or hangings and an epitaphios from the church of the Three Hierarchs. The two tomb covers are in the portrait style of Jeremiah Movila. The embroidered figures have been transfered to a modern background, so that any border there may have been has been lost. The style of the costume is markedly Turkish, and the embroiderer has paid the same careful attention to reproducing the pattern on the brocades. The faces, however, have been worked on applied silk, and are very coarse compared to earlier Moldavian portraiture.

68-70   The veils from the Three Hierarchs are excellent examples of the new fashion for wide decorative borders based on oriental flower designs. The epitaphios, apart from the border, is archaistic in style, showing the figure of Christ on a starry background with no stone and no mourning figures, but only a group of angels and the Evangelists in the corners. The podeai or hangings have St. Peter, St. Paul, the Three Hierarchs (St. Basil, St. Gregory Nazianzene, and St. John Chrysostom), St. Nicholas, an Annunciation and an Anastasis. These too have rich floral borders and initiate the habit of scattering the ground with Persian-style flower studies which was to become so prevalent in the next century. The figure drawing is somewhat stiff and formal and has already lost the strength of the earlier period.

Early in his reign, at the end of the 1630's, Basil the Wolf commissioned icons for the church of the Three Hierarchs from Moscow, and also sent artists to Moscow to obtain permission to make a curtain (katapetasma) in the Russian manner. Such a curtain was evidently received from Moscow with the icons, but it is not clear whether this is one of the existing ones.[96] It seems more likely that these were made at Jassy but influenced by the ' Russian manner ', which can be seen in the style of the Annunciation, the portraits of the Three Hierarchs and the attenuated height of the figures. Russian artists were also brought to Jassy to decorate the church.

This group from Jassy virtually brings to a close the story of church embroidery in Moldavia. In Wallachia events followed much the same pattern.

The Wallachian princes of the fourteenth century modelled their court and civilization on Byzantium. In 1359 a metropolitan consecrated by the Patriarch at Constantinople took office, and towards the end of the century the earliest

[96] N. Grigoraş, Biserica Trei Ierarhi din Iasi, 1962, pp. 31-32.

monasteries were founded by a Serbian monk named Nicodemus, who came to Wallachia from the Athonite monastery of Chilandari. His disciples were also responsible for the Moldavian monastery of Neamţ, built in 1392. His first Wallachian foundation was Vodiţa, which has since been destroyed, but it was found to be uncomfortably open to Hungarian attack, and was replaced in the 1380's by Tismana, built in a more secluded position.

From Tismana there survive a fine late fourteenth century stole with saints and prophets in linked circles, and an epigonation with the Anastasis,[97] but it is generally agreed that these could not have been made in Wallachia at this early date and are probably Greek.

Wallachia had acknowledged the suzerainty of the Sultan as early as 1396, but the princes contrived to retain a degree of independence. The establishment of embroidery workshops was probably at least partly due to Moldavian example, but the embroideries that survive are neither so numerous nor so accomplished. The earliest of them is the epitaphios of Cozia, dated 1396. It is one of the first [101] known epitaphioi to include the figures of the Virgin and St. John, but in spite of this move away from the purely liturgical meaning, it is extremely hieratic in style. Four deacon-angels of remarkably severe aspect stand guard in the background, and there is none of the warmth of emotion expressed by the angels in the Euphemia epitaphios and its Moldavian copies, or even Salonica. The [97, 95] broad band of ornament, highly Islamic in style, below the bier is also unusual. It has been suggested that this epitaphios was made to a design from Mount Athos,[98] which may be so. It is like nothing else in Rumania, but does not suggest Byzantium either.

Although no major pieces of Wallachian embroidery survive between this and the end of the sixteenth century, it is clear that workrooms flourished. Many gifts were sent by the princes to the monasteries of Mount Athos. In Rumania there is a stole at Govora[99] from the time of Radu the Great (1495-1508), one from Tismana[100] from the early sixteenth century, which is unusual in giving the length of two sections to a very large-scale Annunciation, one from Bistriţa,[101] [42] given in 1521 by Barbu Craiovescu, head of the famous boyar family which founded the monastery. The reign of Neagoe Basarab (1512-21) marked a period of great prosperity and expansion in Wallachia. Neagoe sent gifts near and far, to Serbia, the home of his wife Milica, daughter of the Despot Jovan Branković,

---

[97] Millet, Broderies, pl. I.
[98] Turdeanu, Les étoles, p. 171.
[99] Millet, Broderies, p. 26, pl. LII.
[100] A. P. P. R., Studii, p. 123, fig. 5.
[101] Ibid., p. 120, fig. 4. There are two monasteries of this name in Rumania, one in Moldovia and one in Wallachia.

to Mount Athos, and to monasteries in Jerusalem. His stole at Xenophon[102] is worth mentioning for the corded edging to the stole itself and to the arcades which surrounded the figures. Wallachia had close relations with Italy at this time and Neagoe gave several vestments of Italian silk to Bistriţa. Since corded edgings were a feature of Venetian orphreys at the same period, one must ask whether the Wallachian embroiderers can have copied the idea from a Venetian vestment.

All these are arcaded stoles, but the tri-lobed and pointed Islamic arch seems to have been especially popular in Wallachia. It is also found in Byzantine embroideries but not in Moldavia. As far as ornament is concerned, the stole of Radu the Great, as might be expected, is decorated in the interlaced Arabic style, while the plainer type predominated in the first half of the sixteenth century. Two stoles in Athonite monasteries (Vatopedi and Esphigmenou) were given by Radu Paisie (1535-45), and two oraria from the same reign, obviously from the same workshop, illustrate the broadening of the ornamental style. One of these has the same corded edge as the epitrachilion.[103]

48

The artistic decline towards the end of the sixteenth century is more noticeable in Wallachia than in Moldavia. The large iconostasis curtain of the Crucifixion given to Staneşti by the boyar Stroje Buzescu is a hard and undistinguished piece both artistically and technically, in which only the portraits of the donors seem to have life and reality. Nevertheless the tradition of embroidery lasted rather longer in Wallachia than in Moldavia. Among the last of the important narrative embroideries is the epitaphios of Prince Şerban Cantacuzene, presented to Tismana in 1681. This, and two others like it, are interesting from the iconographical point of view in that they illustrate two parallel scenes, the traditional Lamentation, and the Descent from the Cross, which, though not unknown in Byzantine art, was seldom, if ever, used in embroidery in earlier periods. Technically the Tismana epitaphios is typical of its period. The gold embroidery is highly competent but without refinement, and the earlier method of mingling colour with the gold has gone.

67

111

During the early years of the eighteenth century iconostasis curtains and tomb covers eliminated the figure subject entirely and were decorated with wide ornamental borders which were often Italianate in style.[104]

It is significant that the Wallachian prince, Constantine Brăncoveanu (1688-1714), ordered his embroideries from the leading foreign artist of the day, Despoineta in Constantinople, while in the 1750's his family patronised the Serb designer, Christopher Žefarović.

[102] Millet, Broderies, p. 21, pls. LXXII-VI.
[103] Millet, Broderies, pp. 32, 33, 50, pls. LXXVII-LXXIX, CII, CIII.
[104] A. R. P. R., Studii, p. 135, fig. 25.

During the second half of the seventeenth century the Rumanian principalities completely lost whatever independence they had managed to retain in the face of continuous Turkish pressure. Nominally the two principalities continued in existence. In actual fact the princes were appointed by the Turks, mainly from among the Greek aristocratic families of Constantinople—the Phanariots — and remained to a greater or lesser extent the puppets of their Turkish masters. Economic exploitation and the collapse of the trading conditions which had founded their prosperity reduced the principalities to purely agricultural communities, but the feudal structure was not destroyed, as it was under active Turkish occupation in the Balkans, and the landowners contrived to retain a certain amount of wealth and power. This was a period when the monasteries of Mount Athos, and to a lesser extent the Meteora, relied greatly on the financial support of the principalities and received generous gifts of money and land from the Rumanian princes and boyars. They certainly also received other presents, and it seems likely that the Athonite monasteries own a number of embroideries from this late period given by Rumanian landowners.

The large monastic workrooms, however, which had been the appendages of the princely courts, died with the independence of the princes. We have seen already that some boyar families were ordering embroideries from abroad at the end of the seventeenth and during the eighteenth century. It is also probable that, as in Serbia and Greece, embroidery was carried on in a small way in the Rumanian monasteries or by amateurs.

An eighteenth century epitaphios preserved at Putna[105] must be Moldavian work. It is strongly archaistic in style and quite different from the contemporary ' westernising ' designs of the innovators, with their emphasis on decorative detail. It was obviously copied from the classic Moldavian epitaphioi, but is artistically a sad caricature of the great period.

Although church embroidery suffered a temporary eclipse in Constantinople immediately after the conquest it appears to have revived again by the sixteenth century. A number of Greek works of this period survive which are by no means negligible. There is unfortunately nothing to show where they were made. Probably they were the work of monasteries or convents which had managed to retain their standards, whether they were situated in Constantinople or elsewhere. One such piece is a fine stole with Feasts in the Athonite monastery of

[105] O. Tafrali, Putna, No. 68.

[106] Millet, Broderies, pls. CX-CXII.

the Great Lavra, illustrated by Millet.[106]   It probably dates from the sixteenth century, and since it was the gift of a priest at the Oecumenical Patriarchate, may be Constantinopolitan work. Another is the curtain which is now in Belgrade,

66 signed in Greek by the Nun Agni. It may have been made in Macedonia or South Serbia.

Various embroideries signed by the monk Arsenius at the end of the sixteenth century may have been made in a monastery of the Meteora. The first years of of the seventeenth century produced a fine epitaphios at the monastery of Secu

110 in Moldavia which is actually signed ' by the Nun Philothea of Constantinople ', as well as the omophorion at Grottaferrata which was originally made for an

50 Archbishop of Patras.

Pieces such as these show that embroidery of a high standard was still done in Greece, or the Greek cities of Asia Minor, and in Constantinople itself during the sixteenth century, although the emphasis was on technical efficiency rather than artistic worth. But these pieces were relatively few, and in general changing conditions everywhere meant that embroidery, which had been essentially a highly professional craft, was relegated to the amateur efforts of pious ladies in their homes, or the frequently equally inept work of the small religious house or the semi-amateur single-handed embroideress.

From the sixteenth and seventeenth centuries we also have a series of so-called ' peasant ' epitaphioi from Greece, which were clearly made for village churches and can be compared to the ' peasant ' icons of the same period.

The deplorable decline in standards which these conditions had brought about by the turn of the seventeenth century fired the two practitioners whose work we have already studied, Despoineta and Žefarović, to make deliberate efforts to bring new life into the craft by importing western ideas. It is clear from the votive inscriptions on Despoineta's work and that of her followers that bourgeois donors in a position to make gifts of some value to churches were not lacking in the Greek towns of Asia Minor and in Greece itself. Despoineta in fact brought a return of technical standards and considerable artistic merit to a period of revival which was to last in the Greek world well into the eighteenth century.

efarović, although his own works are technically impeccable, had less success in raising standards generally. The Patriarchs of Karlovci, driven by the Turks to Austrian-controlled territory north of the Danube from the Serb Patriarchate of Peć in 1690, were particularly concerned to foster artistic and literary talent in their efforts to preserve the national and religious identity of their people. More famous painters than Žefarović, working under their auspices, adapted the traditional Byzantine style to the wave of baroque influence which flooded northern Serbia at this time. In embroidery the baroque and rococo had already penetrated the decoration of some seventeenth century Serbian work in a rather half-hearted way. It was left to Žefarović to handle the style with greater assurance, but although the effect of his work can be seen on later embroideries from this area, his followers descended very soon into the artistic wilderness of the nineteenth century.

This was the period when embroidery throughout all the Orthodox countries of south-eastern Europe reached the lowest possible level, both artistically and technically, from which there was to be no recovery.

CHAPTER TEN

THE PIECES ILLUSTRATED

In discussing the illustrations I have tried to give an idea of the development of these embroideries in general terms, and the relation of the pieces to each other, rather than a complete picture of the known examples, which is to be found, in so far as it exists anywhere, in Millet. I have given in footnotes the main sources only in which each piece has previously been published. These notes are intended for the student who requires fuller information than I have given: they are in no sense a complete bibliography of every piece illustrated. As technique has been very fully dealt with in Chapter VIII, and in any case changes very little, I have not dwelt on technical detail unless a point seemed worthy of particular attention.

Sacci

As far as possible the illustrations are described in the order in which the vestments are listed in Chapter III, but it seemed fitting to start with one of the most splendid examples that the Byzantine fourteenth century has left us, the so-called Dalmatic
1-6   of Charlemagne in the Vatican.[107] It has been recognised now for very many years that this is not a dalmatic, nor has it any connection with Charlemagne. It is quite certainly a patriarchal saccos dating from the middle of the fourteenth century. From the beauty of its design and technique, it was probably embroidered in Constantinople. It first figures in a Vatican inventory in 1489, and may have been brought to the west by refugees after the fall of Constantinople.

It is embroidered in gold and silver with only a little colour on a background of dark blue silk. The metal thread is turned frequently, and the inner drawing is worked in coloured split stitch. There has been some rather crude restoration in the background, and some of the metal thread has been replaced with a plaited braid. The piece at the bottom has obviously been added, but the work is evidently Byzantine and this must have been done before the saccos was brought to the west.

The theme of the whole vestment is Salvation. On the front is a remarkably

---

[107] Millet, Broderies, p. 67ff., pls. CXXXV-CLI; Millet, La dalmatique du Vatican; Mirković, Crkveni Umetnički Vez, p. 32. Braun, La Dalmatique du Trésor de St. Pierre.

fine composition illustrating the Second Coming or the Calling of the Chosen, that is to say a reduced form of the Last Judgment, in which the emphasis is on eternal life and the Damned are omitted. On the back, the Transfiguration foreshadows the glory of the Saviour in Paradise, which will be shared by the faithful at the Resurrection, while the Communion of the Apostles on the shoulders indicates the road to Salvation through the medium of the Eucharist.

The theme of the Second Coming on the front, with all its complex symbolism, has been exhaustively analysed by Millet in *La Dalmatique du Vatican*. In it, Christ is shown as the youthful Christ Emmanuel (Isaiah 7, 14; Matthew 1, 10-23), that is to say the Son of God, the Saviour offering eternal life and the incorruptibility of the flesh after resurrection, rather than the Son of Man, Judge of men. At His head, below the monogram, are the words ' The Resurrection and the Life'. In his hand He holds the open Gospel with the command to the elect: ' Come ye blessed of my Father, inherit the kingdom prepared for you '. (Matthew 25, 34.) Rising in the background the Cross replaces the Prepared Throne, and around Him are the glorifying choirs of angels and the Beasts of the Apocalypse, who give ' glory and honour and thanks to him that sat on the throne, who liveth for ever and ever '. On each side His Mother and St. John intercede constantly for the faithful, and at His feet the Chosen, emperors, hierarchs and saints, offer in their turn their hymn of praise and intercession.

In the lower corners Abraham and the Good Shepherd are shown outside the main scene.

The dramatic representation of the Transfiguration on the back follows the twelfth century commentators on the biblical texts, who enlarged on the separate reactions of the three Apostles. Two subsidiary scenes are included, showing Christ leading the disciples up and down the mountain.

This is the finest piece of embroidery to survive as far as characterisation in faces and attitudes is concerned. The balanced elegance of the composition and the grace of the figure drawing ensure for it a place amongst the greatest monuments of late Byzantine art.

Two very fine Byzantine sacci are connected with the Metropolitan Photius of Moscow (1408-1432).[108] Both have figure embroideries worked in crosses, 7-14 circles and ' gamma ' shaped pieces which are applied to a background of blue silk. On both, these embroideries are framed in a narrow border, front and back, in which the text of the Creed is worked in Greek.

The so-called Great Saccos has on the bottom at the front portraits of 7-10 Vassili Dmitrievitch, Grand Prince of Moscow, and his wife Sophia Vitovtovna,

---

[108] Museum of the Moscow Kremlin, Palace of Arms, Pamatniki Vizantiiskogo Iskusstva, V-XV Vekov, pp. 28, 29, figs. LVI-LXVII.

with their daughter Anna Vassilievna and son-in-law John Palaeologus, the future Emperor John VIII. It is clear that the saccos was sent to Moscow as a present during the brief period between John's marriage to Anna Vassilievna in 1416 and her death in 1418.

On the same side the Crucifixion is illustrated in the upper cross, with prophets in roundels in the angles of the cross, and the Prophets Isaiah and Jeremiah at full length at either side of the horizontal arm. The Annunciation (above) and the Entry into Jerusalem (below) occupy the corner pieces.

In the lower cross the Anastasis is depicted, with prophets in roundels and the Emperor Constantine and Empress Helena on either side. The Last Supper and the Washing of Feet are in the corner pieces. Below the cross three Lithuanian martyrs are shown, in deference to the Princess Sophia Vitovtovna, who was a Lithuanian by birth.

Between the two crosses the Body of Christ is lying beneath a ciborium.

At either side of the main scenes are vertical bands with saints in arcaded sections in the manner of a stole. The Metropolitan Photius is shown at the bottom on the left. The lower side sections of the saccos contain the Sacrifice of Abraham and Jacob's ladder.

On the reverse side of the saccos, the Ascension is shown in the upper cross, with two prophets in roundels and Malachi and Micah on each side of the horizontal arm. In the angles are the Flight into Egypt, the Fall of the Idols, the Nativity, the Salutation, the Waking of the Apostles in the Garden of Gethsemane, and the Betrayal. Above the cross is the Hospitality of Abraham.

In the lower cross is the Dormition of the Virgin with saints in roundels and at the sides. The scenes in the corner pieces are the Baptism and the Raising of Lazarus above, and Pentecost below.

Between the two crosses is the Transfiguration. Saints in arcades frame the sides, as they do on the front.

All the inscriptions are in Greek, with the exception of the titles of the Grand Prince and Princess, which are in Russian, obviously as a compliment to them. All the embroidery is outlined in pearls.

II-14 The design and lay-out of the second or 'Little' Saccos is almost identical, but there are no donor portraits. A date as early as the middle of the fourteenth century has been suggested for it, on the grounds of the fine workmanship, and because of the inclusion among the Hierarchs in the vertical borders of Peter, first metropolitan of Moscow, who was canonised in 1339.[109] There is, however, no reason why Peter should not have been included as a compliment to the Russians

---

[109] Museum of the Moscow Kremlin, op. cit., p. 9.

at a later date, and the two sacci are so alike that it seems more likely that they were made at approximately the same period.

The Little Saccos has on one side the Crucifixion in the upper cross, and the Anastasis in the lower cross, with prophets in the angle pieces. In the crosses on the sleeves are the Entry into Jerusalem and Pentecost.

On the reverse side is the Transfiguration in the top cross and the Ascension in the lower one, with prophets in the angles, as there are on the front. In the crosses on the sleeves are the Raising of Lazarus and Christ with the Emperor Constantine and the Empress Helena (a reminder of their part in putting down the Aryan heresy).

The vertical borders contain Evangelists, Apostles, Hierarchs and other saints in arcades.

The saccos has been repaired at the sides with a ribbon with an Arabic inscription, ' There is no god but God '.

Both sacci have had borders of circles and small crosses in seed pearls added at a later date.

A saccos worked some three hundred and fifty years later was designed by the Serb, Christopher Žefarović, for the bishop of Hungro-Wallachia, Neophytos the Cretan, in 1751.[110] On one side are representations of the Annunciation and Christ Pantocrator in arcades with baroque ornament, with figures of the Apostles in medallions. On the other is a Tree of Jesse with figures of the prophets in medallions, surrounding a representation of the Virgin and Child in an arcade. The whole is sumptuously decorated in gold and silver with baroque ornament and flowering stems which make a very handsome vestment. The Tree of Jesse was a common subject for sacci in the seventeenth and eighteenth centuries.

Mitres

The two mitres illustrated show the earlier style in the shape of a plain circular cap, and the higher rounded type which later became fashionable. This shape was to be greatly exaggerated in the later eighteenth and nineteenth centuries.

The mitre at Patmos[111] has been much restored. The embroidered Feasts round the side probably date to the late sixteenth or seventeenth century. The Crucifixion is illustrated. The other scenes are the Entry into Jerusalem, the Raising of Lazarus, the Anastasis and the Doubting of Thomas. A figure of Christ dressed as a bishop and blessing with both hands on the flat top of the mitre is of later date.

[110] Catalogue, Hristofor Žefarović, 1961, p. 71, figs. 130, 131.
[111] Clara Rhodos, VII, 1933, No. 19, figs. 82-5.

17   A mitre which was made for the cathedral of Ankara[112] is dated 1715 and thought to be the work of Despoineta, who also made an omophorion and an epitaphios for this cathedral. The Deisis is shown in the lower band, surrounded by ornament. The double-headed eagle, which was used as the emblem of the Patriarchate after 1453, was later permitted on archiepiscopal mitres. The upper band is decorated with the Nativity, the Resurrection (illustrated), and the Ascension in ornamental medallions, alternating with busts of Prophets. The form of the Resurrection, in which Christ is shown stepping triumphant from an open sarcophagus, is borrowed from western iconography.

18   Pl. 18 shows an icon of St. Dionysius the Areopagite painted in 1729. This can hardly be an accurate portrait of Dionysius, who lived in the first century A.D. and was traditionally the first bishop of Athens: equally, a bishop of the artist's own time would have been shown wearing saccos and mitre. The icon, however, anachronistic though it is, gives a very clear picture of the vestments and insignia worn by a bishop in the late Byzantine period. Dionysius is wearing the sticharion with potamoi and epimanikia, phelonion, epitrachilion, epigonation and omophorion.

Epimanikia

The epimanikia illustrated show two distinct styles, both of which were frequently repeated in the sixteenth century. One has figures and scenes in gold against a dark silk background, while in the other the entire background is covered with embroidered ornament, usually in an interlocking geometric pattern, with the figures often framed in arcades. Very tentatively it may be suggested that the plain backgrounds were usually of Greek workmanship, while the ornamental style was more widespread.

19-21   The cuffs in pls. 19-21 are obviously from the same workroom. One shows the Trinity (the Hospitality of Abraham) and the other two the Annunciation.[113] These may be a pair or merely two from the same design. The easy simplicity of the composition, the absence of ornament except for the very plain border, and the severe technical style suggest a date not later than the middle of the sixteenth century.

22-23   The pair with the Annunciation dated 1608 represents a later, and much less sophisticated, essay in the same tradition. The haphazard introduction of flowers as background ornament is typical of the period.

24   It is possible that the cuffs with the Communion of the Apostles from Vintilă-Vodă[114] are also of Greek workmanship. The clumsy technique seems to indicate

---

[112] Benaki Museum, Ἐκκλησιαστικὰ Κεντήματα No. 45, pl. 18/2.
[113] Millet, Broderies, p. 58, pl. CXVIII.
[114] A.R.P.R., Studii, p. 125, figs. 10, 11.

that they should be dated late in the sixteenth century. The coarse treatment of the drawing lines, which are worked in silver, produces an unusual effect. It seems likely that a Wallachian workroom would have used Slavonic for the inscription at this period, instead of the Greek Πίετε ἐξ αὐτοῦ πάντες (Drink ye all of this).

The cuff from Govora[115] (first half of the sixteenth century) is one of a pair showing the Annunciation. It is Wallachian, and a fine example of the decorated background type. The Slavonic title Blagoveštenie (the Annunciation) is divided between the two cuffs. The silver ornament is interspersed with rosettes in coloured silk.   25

Two details of another pair of Wallachian cuffs with the Annunciation, from the monastery of Bistriţa,[116] are coarser work in the same style.   26, 27

An eighteenth century cuff shows how sadly technical standards had deteriorated in much work of this time, but it nevertheless has a certain decorative charm. A great deal of *tir-tir* (bullion) is used in the floral ornament, which is very typical. The padded satin stitch in silk used in the figures would not be found in earlier work. The choice of subjects would also have been unlikely for epimanikia of an earlier date. The Salutation, which is shown on the piece illustrated, is paired with the Agony in the Garden on the other cuff.   28

Epitrachilia

The oldest stole illustrated came from the monastery of Bistriţa (Moldavia), and dates from the first half of the fifteenth century.[117] The Monastery received many gifts from Alexander the Good of Moldavia and his sons, but the stole has no inscription which gives an indication of its origin. It is decorated with the scenes of the great Feasts framed in linked circles. The usual twelve Feasts are illustrated, with, in addition, the Via Dolorosa, the Spice-bearing Women, the Resurrection and the Doubting of Thomas. The ornament of dragon heads entwined with heart shapes and the sinuous vegetable ornament in the bottom panels, as well as the framework of linked circles and the whole technical style, suggest Greek workmanship, whether it was made in a Greek city or by emigrant workers in Moldavia. The titles of the scenes are in Greek but at this period this is not necessarily a reliable indication of its origin.   29, 30

The background of red silk has been entirely covered with gold embroidery, but the gold thread was turned frequently, and the channels thus reserved allow

[115] Millet, Broderies, p. 61, pl. CXXII.
[116] A.R.P.R., Studii, p. 126, figs. 12, 13.
[117] Millet, Broderies, p. 6ff., pls. V, VI, XIII-XVII; Catalogue, Rumanian Art Treasures 1965-6, No. 23; Turdeanu, Les étoles, pp. 39-40.

the background material to show and lend a rosy tone to the whole work. Probably many more of the drawing lines were originally filled with back stitch in black, as some of them still are, but some may have been left blank in order to create this warm effect. A very small amount of green and blue silk has been used with the gold. The work has the authentic shimmer of pale colour blending imperceptibly with the silvery tones of the metal threads which is associated with the Salonica epitaphios.

31-34   Another stole from the treasury of the monastery of St. John the Divine at Patmos is probably of the same period and certainly of Greek workmanship. This shows Christ blessing on the neck, the Virgin and St. John the Baptist forming a Deisis, saints and Apostles. The circles have already given way to rectangles divided by bands of ornament. Lion masks and animal heads, especially when used in this way rather than as capitals to pillars, seem to have been essentially a feature of Greek embroidery. The double-headed eagle indicates a connection with the imperial house or with the Patriarchate in Constantinople. This is a stole of very fine workmanship, in gold and silver subtly coloured by the use of *chryssónima* and drawing lines in coloured split stitch.

35, 36   The stole shown in pls. 35 and 36 was the gift of Stephen the Great of Moldavia and his son Alexander, whose portraits appear in the lowest panels (not illustrated).[119] Alexander was Stephen's eldest son who died in 1496 before he succeeded to his father's kingdom. Since no wife is mentioned in the dedication it seems likely that the stole was made in the period when Stephen was a widower, between the death of Maria of Mangop and his marriage to Maria Voichiţa, that is between the years 1478-1480.

The usual twelve Feasts are illustrated, but the Ascension has been omitted, while the Last Supper, Gethsemane, the Via Dolorosa, the Flagellation and the Lamentation have been added. The order of the Feasts has been confused. The titles are in Greek, and the brief dedication in Slavonic.

This stole shows the transition from the linked circle to the rectangle and is a good example of the move towards a more geometric ornament. It is considered by Turdeanu to mark the watershed between the 'old' and the 'new' phases in the Putna workroom. It is true that, with the exception of the tomb cover of Maria of Mangop, all the great pieces at Putna were made after this date. It is clearly a Moldavian descendant of two earlier stoles, the one at Bistriţa and one unfortunately now lost, presented by Alexander the Good to Neamţ. (Millet, *Broderies*, p. 6, pl. VIII.) Many writers have remarked that iconographic details

[118] Clara Rhodos, Vol. VII, 1933, No. 1, figs. 10, 12, 14-24; Catalogue, Byzantine Art, 1964, No. 592.
[119] Millet, Broderies, p. 6, pls. XVIII-XXII: Turdeanu, Les étoles, pp. 23-31, pls. I-IV; Tafrali, Putna, No. 96; A.R.P.R., Repertoriul, No. 85, fig. 204; A.R.P.R., Cultura Moldoveneasca p. 484, figs, 3, 4; Jerphanion, Le trésor de Poutna, p. 310-6.

borrowed from the popular art of Cappadocia are to be found in the Stephen the Great stole.

Another Moldavian stole from the reign of Stephen the Great is that given by Stephen and Maria (Voichiţa) to Putna, probably between 1496 and 1504.[120] This has the Deisis on the neck with twelve Old Testament Prophets in arcades on the two panels. We have seen that saints framed in arcades occur in Greek embroidery from the early fifteenth century. The arcaded stoles at Putna were probably copied from examples of Greek workmanship in the monastery. In this stole the lion masks which often formed the capitals of the pillars in Greek arcaded stoles have been dropped and instead a single acanthus leaf springs rather awkwardly from the capital. The prophets are drawn with a good deal of movement, which foreshadows the very active type of the mid-sixteenth century (cf. the curtains of Slatina and the Nun Agni).

37, 39

The technical standard of this stole is high. Comparison between pl. 37 and the two Greek stoles of the first half of the century will help to mark the indefinable change in the technique of laying gold threads which differentiates the fourteenth/early fifteenth centuries from the late fifteenth/early sixteenth. In addition the difference between the colour of the gold and silver thread is more marked in the Moldavian stole, and a great deal of coloured silk is used in the form of *chryssónima*. The dresses of the prophets are gay in red, blue and green against the gold background. The sections are no longer divided by bands of ornament but by plain strips of silver thread worked in a chevron pattern.

The stole at pl. 38 presents a mixture of arcades and plain rectangles, with geometric ornament.[121] Christ is represented between two angels on the neck. There are full length portraits of the Virgin and St. John the Baptist and St. Nicholas and St. John Chrysostom, and busts of eight Apostles. Unusually, some titles are in Greek and some in Slavonic (ὁ Θεολόγος and *Sveti Pavel*). This seems to indicate that it could have been made in either of the Rumanian principalities, or possibly Serbia, but it is difficult to say which. It must date to the end of the fifteenth century.

38

Portraits of donors were common in all forms of Byzantine art, and the saccos of Photius shows that they were not unknown in Byzantine embroidery. Existing examples in embroidery, however, are much more common in Rumania than elsewhere. The first pair illustrated is of Stephen the Great of Moldavia and his wife Maria Voichiţa. The portraits are on a stole given by them to the monastery of Dobrovaţ, probably at the end of Stephen's reign towards 1504. The stole is

40, 41

---

[120] Millet, Broderies, p. 31ff., pls. LXVII-LXXXI; Tafrali, Putna, No. 97, pl. XLIX-L; Turdeanu, Les étoles, pp. 35-36; A.R.P.R., Repertoriul, No. 112; A.R.P.R., Cultura Moldoveneasca, p. 484; Catalogue, Rumanian Art Treasures, 1965/6, No. 26.

[121] J. Braun, Die liturgische Gewandung, p. 599.

worked on dark blue silk and has busts of saints in eight-lobed medallions.[122]

42 The second pair shows the boyar Barbu Craiovescu and his wife Neagoslava, dressed in religious habits. Their stole, which has saints in wide tri-lobed arcades, was given to the monastery of Bistriţa (Argeş region, Wallachia) in 1521.[123] In its present state it looks exceptionally colourful, but this is because the underlay to the gold embroidery was worked in colour. This would not have had a very great effect on the colour of the gold, which was still twisted with a coloured thread, but much of the gold embroidery has worn off, leaving the underlay showing. This is particularly noticeable on the portraits, which now look entirely dark blue.

43 A Moldavian stole of the middle of the sixteenth century now in the Victoria and Albert Museum can be linked with a group of four illustrated by Millet (Broderies, pl. XCV). Three of these have identical stylised flowers in the bottom panels and the fourth can be attributed to the same workroom from the style of the figures. Two of these stoles, one with Feasts and one with figures of saints, are in the monastery of Dionysiou. A third, at Dragomirna in Moldavia, has cherubim in exactly the same style as the stole illustrated here, but alternating with half-length figures of angels. Although the decoration of these two pieces, angels and cherubim, would seem more suited to an orarion (see p. 18 above), they are in fact both epitrachilia. The example illustrated has had the neck cut out at a later date. The four pieces published by Millet can be attributed, through the donors, to a Moldavian workroom of the 1550s. The one in the Victoria and Albert Museum is clearly from the same workroom. It is signed across the bottom panels, ' Master Dmitru of Tetin [124] and his companions made this stole '.

This group of stoles carries the undecorated style to its furthest limit but, as often happens in Moldavian work of this period, ornamental detail is replaced by colour. Both this and the stole at Dragomirna have a large proportion of red, green and blue thread twisted with the gold, as well as red, green and blue split stitch to mark the inner drawing.

44 The linked circle framework for a stole, allied to twining ornament, appears to have remained popular with Greek workers until a fairly late date, while it never found much favour in the Rumanian principalities. (Dobrovaţ is a Moldavian example in this style, although here the circles have become lobed medallions.) The example illustrated, with single half figures in circles, is Greek work and probably dates from the early sixteenth century.[125] Christ Emmanuel is portrayed

[122] A.R.P.R., Studii, p. 156 figs., 5, 6; Turdeanu, Les étoles, p. 33; A.R.P.R., Repertoriul, No. 98, figs., 215-6; A.R.P.R., Cultura Moldoveneasca, p. 485.

[123] A.R.P.R., Studii, p. 120, figs. 4, 6; Turdeanu, Les étoles, p. 46; Catalogue, Rumanian Art Treasures, 1965/6, No. 29.

[124] Possibly the fortress of Ţeţina near Cernauţi.

[125] Millet, Broderies, p. 18, pl. XLI.

on the neck.   Below that Zachariah and St. John the Baptist, the Annunciation, Apostles and Early Fathers.

Three later stoles are illustrated.   Plate 45 shows part of a seventeenth **45** century stole from the monastery of Cotroceni (Wallachia).   The Annunciation is in the first pair of arcades, with St. Peter and St. Paul below.   The titles are in Greek.   The efficient gold technique, combined with the clumsy handling of the drawing (the inner drawing is carried out in laid gold instead of split stitch) is typical of the period.   So is the introduction of the ' Turkish ' carnations and tulips.

The stole from Hurezi was given to the monastery in 1696 by Prince Con- **46** stantine Brăncoveanu of Wallachia,[126] whose portrait, with his family, is shown in the bottom panels. It is one of two sets of epitrachilion and epimanikia signed by Despoineta.   It shows her work at its most decorative, and foreshadows, with its pearls and pale coloured silks, the prettiness which was a feature of Greek eighteenth century embroidery.

The stole by Žefarović is one of a series of almost identical pieces signed by **47** this designer.   The one illustrated,[127] dated 1750, is in the Museum of Art in Bucharest. Others are at Neamţ (1750), Vatopedi (1751) and the Patriarchate at Belgrade (1752), while two more are at Iviron and the Oecumenical Patriarchate in Istanbul.   These stoles are worked entirely in gold and silver with no colours. The ornament, which is purely baroque in style, is heavily padded, and the haloes are worked in a pattern of curving rays which may indicate a Viennese workroom (see p. 63).   The background against which the figures are set is also worked in a pattern of rising curves.

Orarion

Pl. 48 illustrates parts of an incomplete Wallachian orarion of the sixteenth century. **48** The actual pieces are longer than the sections shown in the photograph (1.16m. and 1.19m.), and probably represent about two thirds of the whole.   The word ἅγιος in elaborately decorative lettering alternates with angels officiating as deacons.   The signature in Slavonic in the bottom panels reads: ' John Peter Voivod and his son Mark Voivod in the year 7046 (1538) '.

The name Peter Voivod at this date naturally suggests at first sight Peter Rareş of Moldavia, a bastard son of Stephen the Great who ruled the principality from 1527-1538 and 1541-1546.   It is clear, however, that in this case the donor is Radu Paisie of Wallachia (1535-1545).   Radu Paisie, whose baptismal name was Peter, was a son of Radu the Great.   He took the name Paisie on becoming a

[126] A.R.P.R. Studii, p. 135, figs. 19, 20.
[127] Catalogue, Hristofor Žefarović, 1961, p. 68; Stojanović, Umetnički Vez, No. 66.

monk, and was at one time Abbot of Argeș. When he finally became Voivod in 1535, he also adopted the name Radu, as many Wallachian princes did. His eldest son, who pre-deceased him, was named Mark. He was the founder of several monasteries in Wallachia, and sent gifts to the monasteries of Mount Athos, including two stoles, one at Esphigmenou and one at Vatopedi. (Millet, Broderies, pls. LXXVIII, LXXIX and LXVII, LXXVII.) The stole at Esphigmenou has an identical inscription, with the date 1537.[128] Peter Rareș of Moldavia had three sons, none of whom was called Mark.

The orarion may be compared with another at Iviron illustrated by Millet (Broderies, pls. CII and CIII) and dated 1533, which also has angel/deacons in very much the same style performing the duties of their office. Both these oraria, as well as the borders of a pair of podeai made in Wallachia in the reign of Radu Paisie which are also at Iviron, show the bold yet decorative treatment of ornament which was a feature of their period. (Compare the lettering of ἅγιος in the orarion illustrated with the border of the podeai (Millet, Broderies, pls. CLXXII, CLXXIII).) The same tendency to broad simplification, which was presumably a reaction against the elaborate and sometimes fussy decoration of the preceding century, can be seen in the branches and foliage of the Slatina curtains, which were made in Moldavia some years later.

The orarion is worked largely in silver thread, twisted with coloured silks. An interesting point is that the background is worked in silver with yellow silk, evidently as an economy measure to simulate the appearance of gold. The inscription and patterns are outlined in black.

Omophoria

The crosses, poloi and bands on an omophorion are invariably embroidered separately and applied to the vestment afterwards. This means that early embroidery can be removed and re-applied to a new vestment, and leads to even worse confusion in the question of dating. The crosses on an early omophorion were invariably square. By the late seventeenth and eighteenth centuries they were often more decoratively shaped and purely ornamental, rather than embroidered with scenes.

49   The omophorion at Patmos is probably from the late fifteenth or early sixteenth century.[129] The cross illustrated shows the Anastasis, with the Prophets Job, Ezekiel, Moses and Zephaniah.

50   The omophorion in the Basilian Abbey at Grottaferrata[130]is decorated with the

[128] Millet, Broderies, p. 33; Giurescu, Istoria Românilor II, Part 1, p. 157.
[129] Clara Rhodos, Vol. VII, 1933, No. 10, figs. 64-72.
[130] A. Muñoz, L'art byzantin à l'exposition de Grottaferrata, p. 143, fig. 100.

statutory four crosses containing the Feasts in the following order:

(1) The Nativity with the Annunciation and Baptism.
(2) The Congregation of Saints (οἱ Ἅγιοι πάντες) with the Transfiguration and Entry into Jerusalem.
(3) The Crucifixion with the Presentation in the Temple and the Dormition of the Virgin.
(4) The Resurrection with the Ascension and Pentecost.

The Christ on the neck is shown dressed as a bishop and blessing with both hands. The scenes are titled in Greek, and a Greek inscription states that the omophorion belonged to the Metropolitan Theophanos of Old Patras, and gives the date 1618. It has been argued that because the inscription is in a different style it was a later addition, and that the embroidery itself dated to the thirteenth century. The whole iconographic and above all the technical style, however, make it quite clear that Muñoz is right in saying that the embroidery dates from the same period as the inscription. If the inscription was added to an existing omophorion for the Metropolitan Theophanos, the embroidery was certainly not more than a quarter of a century old at the time.

Epigonatia

We have seen already that the Anastasis was the usual choice for epigonatia of the fourteenth and fifteenth centuries. A very fine example which probably dates to the late thirteenth or early fourteenth century is in the Byzantine Museum in Athens.[131] Unfortunately this piece is very badly worn indeed. Were it not for this, it could be counted among the most beautiful of the surviving embroideries of the Byzantine period.

The iconography is in the normal late Byzantine form. Christ, who bestrides the body of Satan, is holding Adam by the hand and drawing him from his sarcophagus. Eve can be seen behind Adam. On the right of the picture are the two prophet-kings and St. John the Baptist.

The treatment of the faces is very fine indeed: perhaps the only piece that can be compared with it in this respect is the Vatican saccos. The border design, although it consists largely of the Islamic 'half-palmette' which is so common in embroidered borders, is not otherwise found in embroidery in quite this form. It is more usual in manuscripts. The haphazard arrangement of the cross-in-circle device in the background would alone date the piece to the fourteenth or perhaps even the thirteenth century. The fact that the embroidery is worked directly on the background silk with no underlay suggests an earlier rather than a later date.

---

[131] Maria Sotiriou, Πρακτικὰ Χριστιανικῆς Ἀρχαιολογικῆς Ἑταιρίας Β, 1936, pp. 110-111.

Another epigonation which can be dated to the fourteenth century is preserved in the treasury of the monastery of St. John the Divine at Patmos.[132] This piece is described as an epigonation, and since there are tassels on three corners it has evidently been so used, but both the subject and the fact that the scene is set on one side of the square are very unusual, and it is possible that it was made as an aër or sanctuary hanging. (In size it corresponds better to an epigonation — 0.40 x 0.42 m.)

The subject is the Christ Child, watched over by the Virgin bearing a deacon's fan and an angel holding the instruments of the Passion. All of this would accord well with the function of the aër, although no other aër appears to be decorated in this way. It is a good example of the iconographer's habit of enlarging the principal figure (in this case the Christ Child) in accordance with His hierarchical importance and without reference to the relative size of other figures included in the scene. The Sleeping Christ Child is found in frescoes on Mount Athos from the fourteenth century.[133]

By the sixteenth century the Transfiguration had supplanted the Anastasis as the most popular subject for the epigonation. A Greek example from the end of this century or the beginning of the seventeenth has the traditional iconography treated in rather stereotyped form. (Compare the stiff attitudes of the Apostles with the same scene on the Vatican saccos.) The piece is more heavily decorated than many epigonatia with the same scene from the mid-sixteenth century. Inscribed along one side is the signature, the Humble Metropolitan Gregory.

An epigonation in the Victoria and Albert Museum dated 1587 illustrates the Washing of Feet, another scene which was sometimes used at this period (see p. 19 above). This is Greek work, evidently made for a metropolitan of Larissa. The signature of Joasaph Larissis is in a band across the bottom of the picture.[134] The inscription on the border is taken from the troparion for Maundy Thursday and reads as follows: ' The Apostles, being bound together by the bond of love, offering themselves to Christ the Ruler of all things, stretched forth their beautiful

[132] Clara Rhodos VII, 1933, No. 11, fig. 73.

[133] Byron & Talbot Rice, The Birth of Western Painting, pl. 24.

[134] N. I. Iannopoulos ('Επισκοπικοὶ κατάλογοι θεσσαλίας in φιλολογικὸς Σύλλογος Παρνασσός: 'Επετηρίς, 1915, p. 173) lists the metropolitans of Larissa at this period as Joasaph in 1581, Daniel 1581-1590, another Joasaph in 1590 and again from 1593-4. There is evidently a discrepancy here, and the evidence of the epigonation, which is quite clearly dated, seems to indicate that one or other of the Joasaphs must in fact have been metropolitan during some part of 1587. At the same period yet another Joasaph was Bishop of Stagi, a bishopric subordinate to Larissa, from approximately 1573-1602. The name was popular among the clergy of Thessaly in deference to John Uroš, ruler of Thessaly, who became a monk under the name of Joasaph and was one of the founders of the monastery of the Great Meteoron.

feet, preaching peace to all '. (The verse refers to Isaiah 52, 7: ' How beautiful upon the mountains are the feet of him that bringeth good tidings, that publisheth peace '.)

Iconographically this piece follows the normal Byzantine pattern: Christ is shown drying, rather than actually washing Peter's feet, while Peter himself makes a gesture indicating his protest, ' Lord, not my feet only but also my hands and my head ' (John 23, 9). The drawing is commonplace, however, as often happens in embroidery of this period, while the composition is cluttered with scraps of ornament filling every corner of the background. Technically on the other hand the work is good. It is done on a red silk background, largely in silver thread twisted with coloured silk, which is properly handled to give the true appearance of *chryssónima*, that is, of precious metal flushed with colour, rather than of colour shot with a metallic glitter. The drawing lines are in split stitch in coloured silk. It has been suggested that this could be the work of the Monk Arsenius, whose signed embroideries date from this period and who may have worked in a monastery of the Meteora.[135]

An epigonation by Despoineta dated 1696[136] of the Adoration of the Magi combined with the Annunciation to the Shepherds shows very strong Italian influence. The subject itself is presented in western form, since the usual Byzantine version shows the Magi arriving on horseback as a subsidiary episode in the Nativity. The shelter under which the Virgin sits, the naked Child, the Ethiopian King, the attendants and the form of the choir of angels are all markedly Italianate, as is the formal decoration in the four corners. The inscription refers to the adoration and the presentation of gold, frankincense and myrrh, while the signature ' by the hand of Despoineta ' is on the outer right hand border.

Like all Despoineta's work the embroidery is of a very high standard. It is worked in gold and silver on a red silk ground, with the grass foreground on which the scene takes place embroidered in green. ' Tir-tir ' is used for the decoration and some of the details.

Curtains, Hangings, Podeai, etc.

Two large veils from Putna (sanctuary hangings or podeai) show the Ascension and the Dormition of the Virgin.[137] The first measures 1.12 x 1.33 m., the second 1.27 x 1.31 m. Both bear inscriptions naming Stephen the Great as the

---

[135] Catalogue, Byzantine Art, 1964, No. 596.

[136] Benaki Museum, Ἐκκλησιαστικὰ Κεντήματα No. 41.

[137] A.R.P.R., Repertoriul, pp. 294-6, figs. 206-8; A.R.P.R., Cultura Moldoveneasca, pp. 502-3, figs. 26-28; Tafrali, Putna, Nos. 69, 70, pls. XXV, XXVI; Ştefanescu, La peinture religieuse, pp. 53-4, 198-9; Millet, Broderies (Dormition only) p. 81, pls. CLXIV, CLXVII.

donor, and they are dated 1484 and 1485 respectively. The monastery was burnt to the ground in the spring of 1484, and the Ascension must have been made immediately afterwards. The monastery church is dedicated to the Dormition, and this is one of two hangings with this subject, the other having been given by Stephen's son Bogdan in 1510.

These two pieces are part of the series of five hangings or curtains which, together with the epitaphioi of Stephen's reign, substantiate the claim that the Putna workroom developed a recognisable style of its own (see p. 85). The characterisation of faces was handled with care, while keeping strictly within the bounds of Byzantine tradition. Pl. 58 brings out clearly the very free treatment of the laying of the gold threads to produce changes in the play of light. These embroideries already show the marked increase in the use of coloured silk, always to greater or lesser extent mixed with gold or silver thread, which was to become such a feature of Moldavian embroidery in the first half of the sixteenth century. This series is purely pictorial in character. Apart from the border patterns, no decorative element intrudes in the composition. Their narrative style is closer to the frescoes of the period than to the purely liturgical illustration of embroideries such as aëres and epitaphioi. The elongated figures reflect in the mannered elegance of attitude and drapery the sophisticated other-worldliness of late Byzantine art.

59-65 Two later Moldavian curtains which appear to be developed from the Putna style give a very colourful impression. The figures are worked in a wide variety of coloured silks, still twisted with a small proportion of metal thread, against a laid gold background. These are two curtains given by the Voivod Alexander Lăpușneanu and his wife Roxanda to the monastery of Slatina.[138] The larger of the two is dated 1561. The curtains are very similar in design, although the arrangement is slightly different. Both show the Transfiguration. At the top is Christ Emmanuel surrounded by angels. Below, the church is offered by St. Peter and St. Paul to Christ and the Virgin, with the donors in attendance. Two bands with Old Testament prophets, who are shown in lively movement, flank the composition. The larger curtain has a wide border of scrolls of vegetation surrounding the scenes of the twelve Feasts. It has been suggested that the smaller curtain is unfinished and should have had a similar border.

The sweeping treatment of the foliage is typical of the mid-sixteenth century (cf. the orarion, pl. 48), a half-way house between the unadorned pictorial style of fifty years before, and the riot of floral decoration which was to come. The form of the border was undoubtedly inspired by the hanging of the Dormition

[138] A.R.P.R. Studii, pp. 159-167, figs. 10-15; Catalogue, Rumanian Art Treasures 1965-6, No. 30 (small curtain only).

of 1510 (A.R.P.R., Cultura Moldoveneasca, p. 274, fig. 5) which has scenes from the lives of the Apostles enclosed in similar scrolls. This may in its turn have been based on a Byzantine formula for curtains (see p. 77). The Feasts on the Slatina curtain are finely worked and very colourful. Christ preaching in the Temple is substituted for the Transfiguration.

A curtain which has a great deal in common with this pair and, although there is no votive inscription, must date from approximately the same period, is one signed by the Nun Agni, now in the Museum of Decorative Art in Belgrade.[139] This curtain was brought from the monastery of Rača on the Drina in the emigration led by the Patriarch Arsenius from South Serbia across the Danube in 1690. Thereafter it was at the monastery of Beočin until the last war. It is worked on a background of dark red silk, and a good deal of coloured thread is mixed with the gold and silver, although it is not as strongly colourful as the Slatina curtains. The Annunciation in the middle is surrounded by the remaining eleven Feasts, with a border of Old Testament prophets, who are drawn with an even greater wealth of gesture and sense of free movement than their counterparts at Slatina. The iconography of the Feasts is very similar to Slatina, while the Ascension and Dormition may be compared to the large Putna hangings. Even in a small technical detail the curtain resembles Slatina. Hair is worked as usual in split stitch, but instead of alternate lines of stitching in two colours, it is divided arbitrarily into flat bands by lines of dark stem stitch. (This, unfortunately, cannot be seen from the photographs.) In spite of these points of likeness, the whole appearance and technique of this curtain make it clear that this is not Moldavian work. In addition the titles are in Greek. The signature ʺΑγνι Μοναχή appears below the Dormition, but there is nothing to show whether Agni was embroideress or donor.

These curtains seem to emphasize how very widespread were the similarities in the embroidery of any given period. Changes, whether technical or iconographical, were very slow to develop, and often seem to grow from the artistic conventions and technical customs of a period, rather than from any strong regional impetus.

The curtain with the Crucifixion from Wallachia dates from the last years of the sixteenth century.[140] It was the gift of the boyar Stroje Buzescu, who died in 1602, and his wife, to the monastery of Staneşti. This technically uninteresting and artistically arid piece marks a very sharp decline from the standards of the curtains so far considered. Greater care seems to have been exercised on the portraits of the donors than on the figures of the Crucifixion. The designer

[139] Mirković, Crkveni Umetnički Vez, p. 12, pl. II; Stojanović, Umetnički Vez, No. 38, pls. 24, 26, 28.
[140] A.R.P.R., Studii, p. 131, fig. 14.

seems to have made a not very successful attempt to adapt the classic border pattern to the current trend towards Turkish floral decoration.

68-70 In the seventeenth century we return to Moldavia, to a fine set of hangings given to the church of the Three Hierarchs in Jassy by Prince Basil Lupu (the Wolf) early in his reign.[141] They date from the years 1638/9. The complete set included an epitaphios, two long curtains with St. Peter (pl. 68) and St. Paul, and four podeai or sanctuary hangings with the Annunciation (pl. 69), the Anastasis, the Three Hierarchs, and St. Nicholas. There is also a long hanging with purely floral decoration (pl. 70). All are worked in gold and silver on a background of red velvet, with wide floral borders on green velvet.

Par excellence, these hangings illustrate the gulf between interest in the artistic representation of the Christian scene and the desire for rich decoration which was the hallmark of the seventeenth and eighteenth centuries. The figure drawing has already become stereotyped (and this tendency was to increase throughout the century). The exceedingly elongated figures of St. Peter and St. Paul and the Three Hierarchs may have been inspired by Russian icon painters. (Russian influence on these embroideries has already been discussed, see p. 88 above). The pot of lilies in the Annunciation and St. Peter's keys are details of western iconography, although the lilies have been given a markedly Near Eastern appearance.

The very rich, beautifully executed floral borders, as well as the isolated flowers scattered under St. Peter's feet, appear to have been strongly influenced by Persian flower design (see p. 46 above). The borders in particular recall Persian carpets, while the centre of the large hanging (pl. 70) has obviously been copied from a Turkish silk.

71-73 The curtain and podea by Christopher Žefarović[142] show a still stronger leaning to naturalistic flower borders. Both were made for the Brăncoveanu family of Wallachia in 1752. The podea has the Coronation of the Virgin in the centre, an entirely western subject, with six of the twelve Feasts in the border. A companion piece made in the same year for the Basarab family, also of Wallachia, has exactly similar floral decoration surrounding another western subject in the centre, the Virgin in a rose garden.

The artistic style of the two podeai and the Vision of Ezekiel on the curtain is, like all Žefarović's engravings, completely western and strongly influenced by his stay in Vienna. The addition of the words ' in Vienna 1752 ' to the inscription of the Coronation podea make it virtually certain that this piece, and undoubtedly the second podea and the curtain as well, were actually worked in a

---

[141] A.R.P.R., Studii, pp. 167ff., pls. 16-20. N. Grigoraș, Biserica Trei Ierarhi din Iași, pp. 46ff.

[142] Catalogue, Hristofor Žefarović, 1961, pp. 69-70.

Viennese workroom, and indeed the technical style is purely western, in that the figures and scenes are carried out entirely in shaded coloured silk (see the detail of Ezekiel, pl. 62), which gives a more painterly result than the classic Byzantine laid gold. The haloes also are treated in the manner of medieval German embroidery, in a curving pattern which is not Byzantine. The same observations apply to the Archangel Michael (pl. 74), a detail from another curtain by Žefarović. In addition, St. Michael is shown carrying the scales, yet another western detail which was foreign to the Byzantine tradition. **74**

Two Greek icons of St. George and the Dragon, which originally belonged to the cathedral of St. George at Argyropolis in the Pontus (the Turkish Gümuşane), also date from the eighteenth century.[143] These are signed by the Nun Agatha, dated 1729, and by Theodosia Kasymbouri, dated 1731, who, as the inscription states, 'worked as an artist in the city of Trebizond'. Theodosia also worked an epitaphios for the monastery of Soumelá in Trebizond. Both these embroideresses were obviously influenced by, and probably even pupils of Despoineta. Both pieces are in the style of painted icons of their time. **75 76**

Agatha's icon is the smaller of the two (0.35 x 0.25 m.) and artistically the most successful, in that the composition is very much less cluttered. It is beautifully worked in gold and coloured silk on a red silk ground, the horse being worked in silver. The treatment of the ' grass ' under the horse's feet shows a revival of the use of *chryssónima*, and at the same time a new approach to this technique. The hillocks are carefully shaded by means of regulating the amount of gold or green silk which is allowed to show in the twist. Old embroideries worked by this method are not shaded. Although there is virtually no formal ornament, this is an excellent example of the elegantly decorative Greek style of the early eighteenth century.

Theodosia's much larger icon (1.08 x 0.72 m.) has an elaborate border with the Trinity at the top and the symbols of the Evangelists in the corners. Down the sides are the Virgin and St. John the Baptist, two archangels and the four Hierarchs in pairs. The bottom panel contains a votive inscription naming the donors, with Theodosia's signature and the date. In the background of the main composition the king and queen watch the contest with the dragon from the city walls, while the princess waits by the gate. A western detail is the crowning of the saint by an angel. As with Theodosia's epitaphios, the work is technically excellent but the drawing is ungainly.

Apart from Euphemia's famous Laud to Prince Lazar, the only known piece of Orthodox embroidery to consist entirely of lettering is the Nicene Creed in Greek, written out in full on a piece which was probably used as a podea. It is dated 1736, and the floral border is perfectly in keeping with this date. **77**

[143] Benaki Museum, Ἐκκλησιαστικὰ Κεντήματα Nos. 47, 48.

78 The first, and earliest, piece illustrated in this section is the small veil or pall made to cover the face only of Prince Lazar of Serbia, who was taken prisoner and killed after the battle of Kossovo in 1389.[144] The veil is embroidered with the text of the Laud to Prince Lazar written by the Princess Euphemia (see p. 59 above). It measures 0.49 x 0.69 m. and is dated 1402. It was formerly at the monastery of Ravanica. Simple border patterns of this kind, consisting of a scrolling stem with small leaf shapes, were common on embroideries of the Byzantine period.

In general the tomb cover seems to have been used mainly in the Rumanian principalities and in Russia. At any rate it is in these countries that the surviving examples are preserved. Its function was not quite the same as that of the English pall, which covered a coffin before burial, and could therefore be used on many occasions and was not connected with any one person. A tomb cover did in fact cover the tombstone of a person important enough for this honour, the underlying idea being, as always, that the draping of any object with a sumptuous cloth was an act of reverence. The tomb cover was therefore made for a specific person and was frequently decorated with a funerary portrait.

79, 80 One of the finest existing examples is that made for Maria of Mangop, second wife of Stephen the Great of Moldavia, after her death in 1477.[145] Maria, as we have seen, was a daughter of the ruling family of Theodoros of Mangop in the Crimea. She was extremely well connected, being related through her mother to the Palaeologi, and the family tie is emphasised by the double-headed eagle and the monogram of the imperial house in the corners of her tomb cover. Another monogram appears to refer the name Asan which, according to Millet (Broderies, p. 79) was used by Maria, together with the name of Palaeologus, on an icon given by her to Grigoriou, but the name has so far not been satisfactorily explained. The monogram of the Palaeologi is repeated in the arcade. It can be assumed that the piece was made at Putna, where it is still preserved, and the fine clear lettering of the inscription, naming Maria and giving the date of her death, is typical of that workroom.

Maria's elegant and aristocratic appearance is enhanced by the elaborate crown and the long Byzantine 'prependulia' which frame her face. Her dress was presumably copied from an actual dress which she wore. The embroiderer

[144] Mirković, Crkveni Umetnički Vez, pp. 30-31, pl. XIII/1; Mirković, Monahinja Jefimija, 1922; Janković, the Nun Euphemia; Stojanović, Umetnički Vez, No. 7, pl. 3.

[145] Millet, Broderies, pp. 78-81, pls. CLXII-CLXIII; Tafrali, Putna, No. 90, pls. XLIII-V; A.R.P.R., Repertoriul, No. 84, figs. 202-3; A.R.P.R., Cultura Moldoveneasca, pp. 504-6; Stefanescu, La peinture, pp. 51-2, pl. 12.

has taken great trouble to simulate the brocade, which was probably one of the Turkish-influenced Italian brocades of the period. It has been realised in embroidery in silver thread, and green and blue silk twisted with silver, with touches of red silk, and creates the impression of a shimmering stuff of royal magnificence.

Two tomb covers of more than a century later belong to the monastery of Suceviţa, which was rebuilt by the Movila family towards the end of the sixteenth century. The portraits of two brothers of this family who ruled Moldavia in turn are represented on these veils: Jeremiah Movila, Voivod from 1595 to 1606, and Simeon, 1606-1607.[146] Simeon had also been Voivod of Wallachia from 1600 to 1602. While Simeon's is a funerary portrait which appears to have been strongly influenced by the tomb cover of Maria of Mangop, Jeremiah Movila is represented as a powerful man very much alive. The embroidered portrait is very like the one of Jeremiah painted in fresco in the naos of the church at Suceviţa. Both portraits, one of the dead, the other of the living, leave a strong impression of truthful realism.

Both brothers wear a magnificent robe, perhaps the same one, which the embroiderer has again taken great pains to reproduce. In this case the brocade was obviously Turkish, but the embroidery, following a style that was becoming fashionable at the time, is entirely in gold and silver, which is harsh in effect and quite misses the subtle beauty of Maria of Mangop's dress, as well, one must suppose, as that of the brocade it represents. The cypresses and flowers in the backgrounds also mark the fashion for Turkish floral decoration which was to prevail in the seventeenth century. It is interesting to see the old Byzantine border pattern of linked circles and leaf ornament still repeated at this late date. Both inscriptions extol the subject of the portrait. Simeon's, which is dated 1609, states that the veil was the gift of his wife Marguita, who presented other embroideries to Suceviţa, including a stole, epimanikia, an aër and a hanging.

Jeremiah's tomb cover has in the background a crown above the emblem of Moldavia, with the letters EM WM (Eremia Movila, Woewoda Moldaviae). In the right hand corner is the Hand of God blessing above the church, which is decorated with the Hospitality of Abraham and the Anastasis. (It was Jeremiah who decorated the church of Suceviţa, which was dedicated to the Resurrection, with frescoes, but these scenes do not correspond to the actual decoration on the outside of the church.)

These two scenes also appear in the upper corners of Simeon's portrait. Below them are medallions containing the emblems of Moldavia (an ox's head)

---

[146] Tafrali, Suceviţa, p. 211-213, figs. XIX/1; Ştefanescu, La peinture, p. 57; Catalogue, Rumanian Art Treasures, 1965/6, No. 31 (Simeon only).

and Wallachia (an eagle carrying a cross). In Simeon's folded hands is the ceremonial handkerchief which is still placed between the hands of the dead in Rumania. Both these pieces are worked on red velvet backgrounds.

83, 84   Two much less talented portraits which belong to the church of the Three Hierarchs in Jassy date from about the 1650s.[147] These are of Tudosca (Theodosia), wife of Prince Basil Lupu of Moldavia and their son John. Another of Basil Lupu himself is said to have been stolen for the sake of the pearls early in the nineteenth century. Although the faces, which are worked in applied silk with the features superimposed in stitchery, are coarse and inelegant, the portraits are interesting from the point of view of costume, and show how far Turkish fashions had penetrated the dress of the upper classes in eastern Europe at this period. Tudosca wears a feminine version of the Rumanian nobleman's fur bonnet worn by her son.

Aëres

The classic decoration in the Byzantine period for the two veils which covered the chalice and patten was the Communion of the Apostles, given in each kind to six Apostles on the appropriate veil. The conception of the Communion as the liturgical form of the Last Supper was by no means new to Byzantine iconography at the time of the earliest existing embroidered veils. It had been used at least as early as the sixth century in manuscripts and on objects connected with the sacrament (for example, the Riha patten).

85, 86   The earliest pair of veils illustrated is in fact much the earliest Byzantine church embroidery that it is possible to date with any degree of accuracy.[148] They are assumed to have been brought back from the Fourth Crusade by Bishop Krosigk of Halberstadt, who returned to his see in 1205 and presented many Byzantine treasures to the cathedral, including a famous silver patten. In fact the veils are not identified conclusively in the wording of the deed of gift by which the bishop made his donation to the cathedral in 1208,[149] but it nevertheless seems more than likely that they reached Halberstadt by this means. At some later date they were mounted on large pieces of Italian fourteenth century brocade and used as processional banners, hence the use of the German word Fahnen (banners) to describe them.

---

[147] Ștefanescu, La peinture, p. 60; Iorga, Buletinul Comisiunii Monumentelor Istorice VIII 1915, p. 147; N. Grigoraș, Biserica Trei Ierarchi din Iași, pp. 61-63.

[148] The altar cloth with two angels at St. Mark's in Venice may date from the same period (late twelfth century) but this is by no means firmly established. (See footnote, No. 73.)

[149] Quoted in Rohault de Fleury, La Messe, 1883, vol. VI, p. 191.

The long Greek inscriptions have been read by Dölger[150] and are translated in full on p. 54 above. They should be read from left to right along the top border, then vertically down the right hand border, then the left hand, then the bottom, and finally the lines above the picture. At the end of each inscription are the words of the communion service for the appropriate veil: ' Take, eat, this is my Body ', and ' Drink ye all of this, this is my Blood '.

Dölger has tentatively identified the Alexius Palaeologus named in the inscription as the maternal grandfather of the Emperor Michael VIII, who married Irene Angelina Comnena, daughter of the Emperor Alexius III Angelus. Their daughter Theodora was Michael's mother.[151] Taking into account the title Sevastos which Alexius uses in the inscription, he suggests a date between 1185 and 1195 for the embroidery.

The veils are worked on a background of black silk. The high rounded ciborium over the altar occurs again in a similar veil once at Ochrid which is illustrated by Kondakov,[152] but this must have dated from about a hundred years later. The technical treatment of the Apostles' clothing, in which the lines of the inner drawing are handled in such a way that they almost create the effect of brocade, is altogether unusual.

The normal iconographical form of the Communion of the Apostles shows the figure of Christ twice, sometimes standing at one altar, with the Apostles approaching from either side to receive the Bread and Wine. In the Halberstadt veils they approach from His left in both cases.

In another pair of aëres dated to just over a century later, they approach from His right in both cases. This pair was bequeathed to the Collegiate Church at Castell' Arquato (Piacenza) by Ottobone Robario de' Feliciani, Patriarch of Aquileia, who died in 1314.[153] There is no dedicatory inscription on the veils, but only the traditional words of the Communion, in Greek, on each. Although they are undoubtedly of Byzantine origin, an iconographical point to notice is that Christ is approaching the Host to Peter's lips, as in the Roman Catholic rite. In the early years in the Orthodox church, the Bread was placed in the hands of the communicant, and later given by intincture from the chalice.

87, 88

The veils have been mounted side by side on one backing to make an altar frontal.

[150] F. Dölger, Zwei byzantinischen Fahnen im Halberstädter Domschatz, in Beiträge zur Geschichte der Philosophie des Mittelalters, Supplement Band 3, Vol. 2, 1935.

[151] Dölger, op. cit., pp. 1358-9; A. T. Papadopoulos, Versuch einer Genealogie der Palaiologen, 1938

[152] N. P. Kondakov, Makedoniya, p. 272, fig. 186.

[153] Millet, Broderies, pp. 72-3, pls. CLIV-V; Catalogue, Byzantine Art, 1964, No. 583.

89   A fourteenth century aër in the Benaki Museum is worked in gold and silver on a dark blue background which has almost completely perished.[154]   It shows Christ with the chalice standing before an altar under a large ciborium.   The frontal attitude of the Christ recalls the same scene on the Vatican saccos.   In this aër, however, the liturgical and symbolic aspect is still further emphasised by the representation of two cherubim, who take the place of the Apostles.   This appears to be the only known aër where the theme is treated in this way, although cherubim became an accepted part of the iconography at a later date when the Christ Child in the patten was substituted for the scene of the Communion, (cf. a late fourteenth century aër at Chilandari, Millet, Broderies, pl. CLVIII/I).   A Greek inscription in the border has the words, ' This is my Blood of the New Testament which is shed for you and for many for the remission of sins '.

90   The Moldavian aër at Suceviţa,[155] worked on a ground of pale blue silk, is one of a pair given by Stephen the Great to the monastery of Rădăuţi in 1493.   (The companion piece is in the Museum of Art in Bucharest.)   The inscription round the border gives the traditional quotation at rather greater length in Slavonic: ' He gave it to His disciples saying, Drink ye all of this, this is my Blood of the New Testament which is shed for you and for many for the remission of sins '.   The dedication is in the bottom border.   This piece represents a particularly Moldavian style in the treatment of the traditional aër.   A pair at Putna (Tafrali, Putna, Nos. 83, 84, pl. XLI) and one at Rossikon (Millet, Broderies, pl. CLXIX) show the same features in the treatment of the scene, although the background is not embroidered in either case.   By contrast the same subject is handled in a slightly different way in a Serbian aër at Chilandari (Millet, Broderies, pl. CLVIII/2).   A later example in the Moldavian tradition is at Dragomirna, dated 1559.

A feature of Moldavian embroidery which is especially marked in the Suceviţa aër is the use of stripes on the altar covering, and in this case on garments as well, which recall the striped materials of Rumanian peasant weaving.   The draping of the ciborium curtains at the top of the picture is another convention common to the series.

The sacrificial aspect of the Communion had been emphasised by the use of the Christ Child in the patten on the aër (see p. 35 above), at least since the end of the fourteenth century.   It seems likely that another aër at Chilandari (Millet, Broderies, pl. CLVIII/I) dates from this period.   This conception became

---

[154] Benaki Museum, 'Εκκλησιαστικὰ Κεντήματα No. I, pls. I, II; Catalogue, Byzantine Art, 1964, No. 584.

[155] Millet, Broderies, p. 82, pls. CLXV, CLXVI; Tafrali, Suceviţa, p. 213, pl. XVIII/1; A. R. P. R., Repertoriul, Nos. 91, 92, fig. 210; A. R. P. R., Studii, p. 157; A. R. P. R., Cultura Moldoveneasca, pp. 493-4, fig. 14.

increasingly popular, until in the seventeenth and eighteenth centuries it had replaced the Communion of the Apostles as the usual subject for the aër.

An example from the end of the sixteenth century in the Benaki Museum has an unusual border pattern of Islamic design.[156] It is very colourful, and worked on a green background, which is also uncommon. Iconographically, however, it contains the traditional elements of the composition. The Christ Child, who is blessing with the right hand, is laid in a patten in the form of an altar and covered with a veil (the aër). Guardian angels and cherubim are in attendance. Over the top of the patten is the *astériskos* or stiffened hoop which in the Orthodox church serves to hold the veil off the patten (cf. the western pall). Over the Child is the Greek inscription ὁ Μελισμὸς τσῦ Χριστοῦ, (the Partition of Christ).

Epitaphioi

During the Orthodox Liturgy the Gifts of Bread and Wine are carried to the altar in the procession known as the Great Entry. In the fourteenth century the liturgical epitaphios, or Great Aër, was included in this procession with other objects connected with the Eucharist, and carried on the heads of the officiating clergy. The scene is illustrated in the representation of the Eucharist in the apse of a number of churches of the period. Pl. 92 shows a later (sixteenth century) fresco in the monastery church of Kaisariani near Athens, in which angels represent the priests celebrating the Liturgy.

The two earliest known epitaphioi are one which belonged to the church of St. Clement of Ochrid, and one which was the gift of Milutin Uroš, King of Serbia, to an unknown church. Both these date from the period 1280-1320. 93, 94

The epitaphios of St. Clement[157] unfortunately disappeared in the period after the 1914-18 war. Its present whereabouts, if it still exists, is unknown. It is signed Andronicus Palaeologus, who is generally considered to be the Emperor Andronicus II Palaeologus, who ruled from 1282-1328. He was related by marriage to the founder of the church of St. Clement, which was consecrated in 1295.

This is a liturgical epitaphios with the Body of Christ guarded by two angels with fans. There is no indication of either praise or mourning by the heavenly host, but the Evangelists are represented by their symbols, as they are on most epitaphioi, to link the Eucharist with the idea of preparation for the coming Judg-

---

[156] Benaki Museum, 'Εκκλησιαστικὰ Κεντήματα No. 22.

[157] Millet Broderies, p. 89, pls. CLXXVII, CXCII; Mirković, Crkveni Umetnički Vez, p. 15, pl. IV/1; Stojanović, Umetnički Vez, p. 41; Kondakov, Makedoniya, pp. 243-5, pl. IV; Ştefanescu, Voiles, p. 104.

ment. An unusual feature is that the traditional Red Stone of Ephesus is shown as a large high bier instead of the more usual flat slab. The Byzantine cross-in-circle motif is scattered in the background. One corner has been repaired by patching with an aër, which covers the lion of St. Mark.

It is impossible to say whether Andronicus ordered his epitaphios in Constantinople or locally in Macedonia. Both this epitaphios and Milutin's have the border which was to become so widely disseminated, the cross-in-circle linked, not by another circle, but by an intertwined foliate pattern. This border appears to have been very common in embroideries of the fourteenth century associated with Byzantine or Serbian Macedonia, and occurs on the Euphemia/Eupraxia epitaphios, which must have been made in central Serbia and may have been instrumental in introducing the pattern to Rumania, where it was repeated for a very long time. Did the border originate in Macedonia, or was it taken there from Constantinople, perhaps by this very epitaphios? This is a question to which there is as yet no answer.

The epitaphios signed in Slavonic, 'Remember, Lord, the soul of Thy servant Milutin Ureš', is invariably connected with Milutin II Uroš, ruler of Serbia from 1282-1321.[158] Now in the Museum of the Orthodox Church in Belgrade, it was at one time in the monastery of Krušedol in the Fruška Gora, where it was presumably taken by refugees from the Turks.

This is the most severely 'liturgical' of all the existing epitaphioi. It is one of two which are intended to be seen vertically instead of horizontally. (The other is at the monastery of Pantocrator, Mount Athos (Millet, Broderies, pl. CLXXVI/2).) The figure of Christ, although obviously intended to represent His Body in the mystical sense, appears almost to be standing rather than lying, and it is the only known example where an aër is shown covering the Christ as it would cover the consecrated Bread and Wine upon the altar. (When the Eucharist is represented by the Christ Child as Lamb of God, the Child is, on the contrary, always covered by a veil.) No Evangelists are shown, and the theme of glorification, with no trace of sorrow or mourning, is expressed by two cherubim and six angels, interspersed with the thrice-repeated ἅγιος of the Sanctus.

The veil is worked on dark red silk, and with St. Clement, provides the earliest example of the classic border pattern.

95, 96
Frontispiece The epitaphios discovered in the modern church of the Panagia of Panagouda in Salonica by Kondakov in 1900 is one of the greatest of the surviving pieces of Byzantine embroidery.[159] There is no dedicatory inscription of any kind, but

---

[158] Millet, Broderies, p. 87, pls. CLXXVI/1; Mirković, Crkveni Umetnički Vez, p. 15, pl. IV/2; Stojanović, Umetnički Vez, p. 41, pl. I.

[159] Millet, Broderies, p. 94, pls. CLXXXII, CXCIII, CC-CCII, CCIV; Le Tourneau/Millet, Bulletin de correspondance hellénique, XXIX, 1905, pp. 259-268; G. Sotiriou, Guide du

there is general agreement that it dates from the fourteenth century. It is of course impossible to tell if it was made in Salonica or Constantinople.

It is unique in composition, in that the usual subject of the epitaphios, the Body of Christ with attendant heavenly powers and the Evangelists, forms a central section, flanked on either side by panels showing the Communion of the Apostles in each kind, thus emphasising the liturgical significance of the veil and its connection with the Eucharist. It is in fact two little aëres and a great aër united in one piece. For this reason it is unusually long in relation to its width (2.00 x 0.70 m.).

The Body is guarded by the traditional deacon/angels with *rhipidia*, but the element of mourning is already clearly indicated by two additional angels whose expressive attitudes illustrate movingly the words of the troparion, ' the Heavenly Host was amazed '. The theme of praise contained in the same troparion is illustrated by cherubim and thrones (the winged wheels studded with eyes of Ezekiel's vision) below the bier. The feeling of deep emotion translated in movement which is present in the angels is repeated in the attitudes and facial expressions of the Apostles in the two Communions.

Technically the Salonica epitaphios is the touchstone by which Byzantine handling of gold thread embroidery may be judged. At first sight consisting entirely of silvery gold and bluish silver, the extreme subtlety of the colouring, achieved by the play of light on different angles of the metal threads, by twisting metal with silk, mostly blue, and in some places by the use of blue couching threads, only becomes apparent as the work is studied from different view points. The Salonica is the only surviving epitaphios to have the background silk entirely covered with gold embroidery.

The large unadorned crosses in linked circles which make up the border are repeated in a podea at Chilandari which probably came from the same workroom (Millet, Broderies, p. 73 ff., pl. CLVII).

The theme of mourning and horror as well as adoration among the heavenly host is further developed in a late fourteenth century epitaphios from Serbia which, although it is still of the liturgical type, has excluded even the Evangelists, and shows instead the Christ surrounded by as many as twelve angels, four with fans and eight weeping or praising God.[160] The theme is further stressed by a quotation from the troparion for Holy Saturday, ' Seeing the strange sight, the host of angels uttered an unaccustomed cry of anguish, O Word of God '.

97

Musée Byzantin d'Athènes, 1932, p. 133; Ştefanescu, Voiles, p. 103; Catalogue, Byzantine Art, 1964, No. 582; Kondakov, Makedoniya, p. 138ff., figs. 81-84.

[160] Millet, Broderies, p. 99ff., pl. CLXXXV; Mirković, Crkveni Umetnički Vez, p. 20, pi. V/2; Stojanović, Umetnički Vez, No. 5; Ştefanescu, Voiles, p. 107; Tafrali, Putna, No. 64, pl. XXI.

This epitaphios is signed in the lower inscription, ' Remember, Lord, the souls of thy servants the empress of Serbia, Euphemia, nun, with the daughter of the queen of Serbia, Eupraxia, nun '. (The title kaisarissa—empress—is probably used in an honorary sense.) Euphemia is usually taken to be the widow of the Despot Uglješ of Serbia (see p. 58 above) whose name is also connected with the curtain at Chilandari and the embroidered version of her own Laud to Prince Lazar. Eupraxia has not been positively identified: the Greek inscription makes it clear that the name of the nun Eupraxia refers to the queen herself and not to the daughter. The epitaphios must have been made at some time after the battle of Kossovo in 1389, when Queen Milica and Euphemia had retired to the convent of Ljubostinje in central Serbia. It is now in the monastery of Putna in Moldavia, where it was presumably taken by Serbian refugees.

The background of this veil is thickly crowded with flower-like stars, which in embroidery seem to have been a development of the Byzantine cross-in-circle motif. Both this starry background and the attitudes of the angels were taken up by Rumanian embroiderers, probably using this epitaphios as a model, and became features of Moldavian embroidery for many years to come.

98, 99 Two epitaphioi which illustrate the classic liturgical type in its simplest form after the manner of St. Clement are in the Treasury of St. Mark's in Venice and in the Victoria and Albert Museum in London. These two are very alike in spite of minor differences. For example, the guardian angels in the Venice epitaphios stand behind the bier, while those in the Nicholas Eudaimonoioannes in London are shown, less conventionally, standing full length at each end. Venice also has the traditional symbols for the Evangelists, while the other has the four Evangelists themselves.

The St. Mark's epitaphios[161] is usually dated to the fourteenth century. Unfortunately a very thorough restoration was carried out between 1735 and 1757 which, judging by the wording of the inventories, may have saved it from total destruction, but has also so altered the character of the embroidery that no deductions can now be made. All the gold embroidery has been reworked in silk, it has been remounted on a new background and acquired a new border. If there ever was a dedicatory inscription this has been lost.

An interesting iconographical point is the Gospel placed under Christ's arm. It was customary to place the Gospels in the hands of bishops or priests when they were buried, but it does not occur in any other epitaphios.

The Nicholas Eudaimonoioannes epitaphios,[162] which is dated 1407, is very

[161] Millet, Broderies, p. 89ff., pls. CLXXX, CXCIII-V.

[162] Millet, Broderies, p. 89ff., pls. CLXXXI, CXCVI-II; C. Rohault de Fleury, La Messe, 1883, Vol. V., p. 45; A. Wace, An epitaphios in London, Εἰς μνήμην Σπυρίδωνος Λάμπρου, 1935, pp. 232-5; Ştefanescu, Voiles, p. 104.

much worn, but raises some interesting questions. As we have just seen, the two full length angels are unusual. Their somewhat forbidding expressions are apparently intended to indicate mourning, and the theme of praise is omitted entirely. Apart from one or two much later pieces obviously designed in a deliberately archaistic style, this is the last but one of the liturgical epitaphioi, the function of the epitaphios in the Liturgy being by this time related specifically to the Good Friday services. Although it does not illustrate the Lamentation, it is linked with the Crucifixion by two verses, the Honourable Joseph, and the Spice-bearing Women, from the troparion for Good Friday, which are inscribed in the border. (The last known example without the figures of the Lamentation is the lost epitaphios from Żólkiew, dated 1428 (see p. 83 above).)

Along the top border is the dedication, ' Prayer of the servant of God Nicholas Eudaimonoioannes with his wife and children in the year 6915 (1407), indiction 15 '. We have seen earlier that the family of Eudaimonoioannes (sometimes also called Daimonoioannes or Monoioannes) as archons of Monemvasia held a prominent place in the history of the Morea from before the Frankish conquest until the final capitulation to the Turks. [163] When the Emperor Manuel II visited the Morea in 1415-16 to put its affairs in order, a member of this family called Nicholas acted as his ambassador to the Venetians in 1416, and in subsequent years conducted diplomatic negotiations between Theodore II of the Morea and Venice.[164] He also acted as one of the Emperor's delegates to the Council of Constance, and played a leading role in persuading Pope Martin V that the Emperor was serious in his desire to reunite the two churches, negotiations which eventually led to the convening of the Council of Florence to discuss this problem.[165] Nicholas himself died before the Council of Florence met, on 1st November 1423. It seems more than likely that this Nicholas is the donor of the epitaphios. It is perhaps worth noting that 1407 was the year of the accession of Theodore II to the Despotate of the Morea, possibly a propitious moment for the presentation of gifts to churches. Another member of the family, George, held an official position at Theodore's court.

In the middle of the eighteenth century we learn from Cajetani, writing in Naples in 1756, that the epitaphios had been since 1628 in the monastery of the SS. Apostoli in Naples, and that it had reached the monastery from Calata in Sicily (which place of this name in Sicily is not clear).[166] It was presumably taken to Sicily by refugees from the Turkish occupation of the Peloponnese.

---

[163] W. Miller, The Latins in the Levant, 1908, pp. 98, 510.
[164] D. A. Zakythinos, Le Despotat grec de la Morée, 1932, pp. 169, 188.
[165] Joseph Gill, The Council of Florence, 1961, pp. 20ff., 27, 29, 30.
[166] Quoted by Rohault de Fleury, loc. cit.

Although it is badly worn and faded the epitaphios is well embroidered. The background pattern of scrolling stems ending in leaf motifs is not uncommon in Byzantine silver, but does not occur elsewhere in embroidery.

101 The epitaphios from the monastery of Cozia[167] in Wallachia may be the first existing example to make the transition from the liturgical style to the illustration of the Lamentation. (It is possible that the Syropoulos epitaphios preceded it, see p. 80 above. There is also a slight doubt regarding the reading of the date of Cozia. This is almost certainly 6904 (1396), but wear on the final *delta* has caused some scholars to read 6930 (1422).) In spite of the fact that the figures of the Virgin and St. John are bowed in sorrow over the bier, this epitaphios remains hieratic in feeling. Even though the Virgin embraces the Body of her Son, the evident emotion expressed by the angels of Salonica is missing. This impression is heightened by the four guardian angels in the background, attired in imperial robes to emphasise their function as attendants on the King of Kings. Rather surprisingly the Evangelists have been omitted.

The background material, now much destroyed, was of dark blue silk. The titles are in Greek, and the Slavonic inscription in the border is from the troparion for Holy Saturday from the Liturgy of St. Basil. There is no dedication. Turdeanu has explained the deep frieze of Islamic ornament below the bier as a misunderstood representation of a much deeper Stone, as in St. Clement. He has also suggested that the design may have originated in an Athonite monastery. A point worth noting in this connection is that Mary is leaning forward to embrace the Christ, rather than holding His head in her lap (see p. 39).

102-4 The epitaphios of Neamţ[168] in Moldavia was given to the monastery in 1437 by the Abbot Siluan, as the Slavonic inscription in the border shows.[169] This is another early representation of the Lamentation with only two figures, which in this case, unusually, are the Virgin and St. Mary Magdalene. This is the first instance in which the Virgin sits at the head of the bier, instead of leaning over from behind it, and the later Moldavian epitaphioi all followed this lead.

This piece seems to have been developed from a Moldavian epitaphios of of 1428 formerly in the monastery of Żólkiew in Poland (see p. 83 above), and both, especially Neamţ, were evidently based on an earlier Byzantine type such

[167] Millet, Broderies, p. 104, pl. CLXXXVII; A. R. P. R., Studii, p. 119; Turdeanu, Les étoles, p. 17.

[168] Millet, Broderies, p. 105, pl. CLXXXVIII; A. R. P. R., Studii, p. 119; Turdeanu, Les étoles, p. 17.

[169] In this case also the date has been queried and read as 1441 by some scholars. The reading depends on the assumption that the final *epsilon* in 6945 (1437) was intended as *thita*, making 6949 (1441), but has worn away on one side. A glance at the laying of the gold thread, however makes it quite clear that *epsilon* was always intended.

as the epitaphios of Bačkovo (Millet, Broderies, pl. CLXXIX). The fine drawing of the Evangelists, the expressive attitude of the mourning angel, the crosses in the background, all point to the designer's familiarity with Byzantine work. These two Moldavian examples are the first to introduce the exclamation preceding the Sanctus to the arcs surrounding the Evangelists.

The brown silk background of Neamţ has been replaced by an eighteenth century restoration in red embroidery, which, because of the variegated colouring and the intrusive nature of the stitchery, detracts seriously from the original intention to contrast the shaded gold of the figures with a plain dark ground. The laying of the gold, in the angels in particular, is carried out with great finesse with a view to exploiting the play of light.

A small veil at Vatra-Moldoviţei[170] (small, that is, in comparison with the Moldavian epitaphioi: it measures 0.69 x 0.63 m.), dating from the time of Stephen the Great, is inscribed in the border, after the quotation ' The honourable Joseph ', ' This Aër was made under the Abbot Pope Anastasius in the year 6992 (1484) May 15th '. It can be regarded as a processional aër or liturgical epitaphios, and for this period is strongly archaistic in style. The Body of Christ lies amid stars surrounded by weeping angels and glorifying cherubim and thrones crying Holy, holy, holy, (the Slavonic *Sveti*). Stone, mourners and Evangelists are all omitted. The drawing of the angels is stiff and ungainly compared with those of the epitaphioi donated by Stephen the Great. As with Neamţ, the background has been restored in red silk embroidery.

Stephen the Great was the donor of three large epitaphioi which were presumably made at Putna. These three, dated 1490, 1494, and 1506, all show the combined influence of Euphemia and Eupraxia and Neamţ, while the iconography of the Lamentation is developed to include more figures. They in their turn acted as models for a series of Moldavian epitaphioi in the sixteenth century.

The latest of these was given to the monastery of Dobrovaţ, and completed in 1506, two years after Stephen's death.[171] It can be seen to have inherited the Evangelists with their liturgical inscriptions from Neamţ, and the angels and star-filled background from Euphemia. (In fact the angels are already a little stereotyped, and are treated with greater grace of movement in the pieces of 1490 and 1494 — Millet, Broderies, pls. CLXXXIX and CXC.) The Virgin is shown standing at Christ's head instead of sitting, St. Mary Magdalene has been joined

[170] Millet, Broderies, p. 87ff., pl. CLXXVII; A. R. P. R., Repertoriul, No. 87; A. R. P. R., Cultura Moldoveneasca, p. 490, figs. 8, 9; Ştefanescu, Voiles, p. 106; Ştefanescu, La voile de calíce brodée de Vatra-Moldoviţei, Art Byzantin chez les Slaves, Les Balkans I, 1930, p. 303.

[171] A. R. P. R., Studii, p. 155; A. R. P. R., Repertoriul, No. 100; A. R. P. R., Cultura Moldoveneasca, p. 497, fig. 20; Catalogue, Rumanian Art Treasures, 1965/6, No. 28.

by another woman, and St. Joseph of Arimathea holds Christ's feet, while St. John stands behind him. The chequered cloth on the bier suggests the influence of peasant weaving which is found quite often in the Moldavian church embroideries of this period. There is a tendency to clutter the background, and the nondescript vegetable ornament crowded between the stars is to appear again in a later epitaphios given by Stephen's son, Peter Rareș, to the monastery of Dionysiou in 1545 (Millet, Broderies, pl. CXCI).

The Dobrovaț epitaphios has also unfortunately lost the whole of its original brown silk background, and now only the linen backing can be seen. The long dedicatory inscription fills the whole border, as it does on all Stephen's epitaphioi (see p. 54 for a translation of the inscription of the Moldovița epitaphios of 1494), and mentions Stephen's son and heir, Bogdan, and his wife Maria (Voichița). The elegant Slavonic lettering is typical of the Putna embroideries.

108-110 Two pieces which illustrate the later development of Stephen the Great's epitaphioi are those from the monasteries of Slatina, dated 1556, and Secu, dated 1608. Both have their full complement of mourning figures, and in both the Virgin is supporting not only Christ's head but His shoulders in her arms. This last iconographical detail was adopted in nearly all epitaphioi from the second half of the sixteenth century onwards (cf. the Greek epitaphios of Theodosia Poulops of 1599, Benaki Catalogue No. 20), and tended to be exaggerated as time went on, so that in late epitaphioi Mary is sometimes seated actually on the bier cradling the whole of the Saviour's head and shoulders in her lap.

The Slatina epitaphios[172] was given by the founder of the monastery (who also gave the curtains already discussed, pls. 59-63), the Voivod Alexander Lăpusneanu and his wife Roxanda. The one at Secu[173] was also given by the founder, a boyar called Nestor Ureche. In both cases this information, with the date, is contained in a long dedicatory inscription filling the border. Both have a second, almost identical, ornamental border of the classic pattern. The Secu epitaphios, which is embroidered on a background of red velvet, has a very small inscription on the lower edge below the frame, stating that it was embroidered by the Nun Philothea of Constantinople. Ștefanescu has suggested that it must nevertheless have been worked from a Moldavian design,[174] and this may well be true.

Greek epitaphioi of this period, however, were less cluttered with extraneous detail, and the Greek workroom may well have saved it from the plethora of stars, flowers and foliage which crowd the background of Slatina. In this the latter may be compared both to Dobrovaț and the epitaphios of Peter Rareș at

---

[172] A. R. P. R., Studii, p. 159.
[173] Ștefanescu, La Peinture, p. 58.
[174] Ștefanescu, loc. cit., note 4.

Dionysiou. The Cross with the Crown of Thorns, the Spear and the Lance and the angel holding the nails appear for the first time in Moldavia in the Peter Rareş epitaphios, and are copied in Slatina. The Cross behind the bier, without the Instruments of the Passion, had been known in the iconography of the embroidered epitaphios since the Syropoulos at Chilandari (probably early fifteenth century), but was by no means unknown in other media then.

Among the last of all the Rumanian embroideries are three epitaphioi from the same design from the end of the seventeenth century. The one illustrated here was given by Prince Şerban Cantacuzene of Wallachia to the monastery of Tismana in 1681 and is now in the Museum of Art, Bucharest.[175] The other two were given to Cotroceni and the Princess's Church in Bucharest, which was founded by the wife of Şerban Cantacuzene.

These are the only examples which combine two scenes, the Deposition and the Lamentation, in the epitaphios, and the result is an unhappy overcrowding in spite of the large size of the veil (1.88 x 1.30 m.). It is also unusual to find portraits of the donors on an epitaphios, although common enough on other pieces. A border of saints and angels in medallions was frequently a feature of Russian epitaphioi, and here may possibly be due to Russian influence.

The work is carried out in gold and silver on a red background with the mechanical competence often found in the seventeenth century. For its period it is unusually free of floral decoration.

Also from the seventeenth century is a much less sophisticated piece, which is typical of a number of embroideries of this period which can be linked with popular art.[176] This is Greek work. It is undated, but the donor is named as Syrianothomas. The scene is given a lively sense of drama by the naive but forceful and realistic attitudes and expressions of the figures. It is worked on a ground of dull yellow silk to give an all-gold appearance. The flowers in the border are in gold and blue.

Despoineta's earliest known work, and perhaps her finest, is the epitaphios given to the cathedral of Ankara by one George, son of Kyriazis, in 1682.[177] Two borders contain the dedication and quotations from the Good Friday troparia.

This piece is worked on a background of dark blue silk in gold and silver and gold-coloured silks. There is very little colour, except for some green below the bier and in the two trees, and some touches of red and pink in the flowers of the border. Despoineta was an extremely talented embroideress who adapted the

[175] A. R. P. R., Studii, p. 133, figs. 17, 18; Catalogue, Rumanian Art Treasures, 1965/6, No. 32.
[176] Benaki Museum, Ἐκκλησιαστικὰ Κεντήματα No. 24.
[177] Ibid. No. 39.

traditional techniques to recreate some life in the stereotyped work in metal threads which was so often produced in the seventeenth century. She employed a wide variety of couching patterns which were unknown in the Byzantine period, and made free use of twisted and plaited gold or silver threads to carry out the inner drawing, and for haloes, edgings, etc. Her angels' wings are worked in silk to emphasise the feathery effect. Her characterisation of faces was excellent, but she achieved this, not with the traditional split stitch, but by shading with coloured floss silks in long and short stitch, a method which she may have learnt from Italian work. For this she used shades of cream and old-gold, which produced the gold-coloured complexions which were a characteristic of her work.

The ciborium had been used in the epitaphios from the beginning of the seventeenth century (M. Beza, Byzantine Art in Rumania, 1940, pl. 19). Despoineta used it in all her epitaphioi, clearly as a means of recalling the liturgical as well as the mourning aspect of the veil, and it was widely used by her followers from this period onwards.

115 It has been mentioned already (p. 61) that two epitaphioi exist worked by Despoineta and her pupil Alexandra. These two pieces are very much alike. The earlier of the two, now in the Victoria and Albert Museum, has a very badly worn inscription at the bottom, which mentions the names of a group of donors, with the date 1712. At the end is the signature, $E\pi ov\acute{\eta}\theta\eta$ $\delta\iota\grave{\alpha}$ $\chi\epsilon\iota\rho\grave{o}\varsigma$ $\Delta\epsilon o\pi(o)\iota v$ $(\acute{\epsilon}\tau\alpha\varsigma)$ $A\rho\gamma\upsilon\rho\alpha\acute{\iota}(\alpha\varsigma)$ $\kappa(\alpha\grave{\iota})$ $A\lambda\epsilon\xi\acute{\alpha}v\delta\rho(\alpha\varsigma)$ (Worked by the hand of Despoineta Argyraia and Alexandra.) It is worked on a background of red silk, largely in silver thread with some gold, with some blue and green silk twisted into the ' grass ' and the dresses. The angels' wings and the flowers are worked in silk in yellow, blue and green. Some ' tir-tir ' has been used for details. It has been mounted on a larger piece of silk at a later date and finished with a fringe. It is possible that there was once a border which has been lost.

Certain features mark this as a product of Despoineta's workroom, the compact group under the ciborium, the standing angels at either end, the flowers (cf. the two trees in the epitaphios of 1682), the working of the angels' wings, and the treatment of the haloes. At the same time the embroidery is not as fine as much of her work, and one is led to believe that Alexandra played a large part in the making of this piece.

116, 117 The epitaphios worked by Theodosia Kasymbouri of Trebizond[178] was given to the Soumelá monastery by the Abbot Sophronius in 1738. (The date is actually embroidered as 1538, but this is obviously a mistake.) This information is contained in a panel in the bottom border. A liturgical inscription forms the inner border.

[178] Benaki Museum, 'Εκκλησιαστικὰ Κεντήματα, No. 51.

Like Despoineta, who obviously exerted considerable influence on her work, Theodosia elaborated on the traditional techniques to obtain her effects. The gold ornament on the dress of the Archangel Michael and on Joseph of Arimathea's ' fair linen cloth ' would have been impossible in earlier centuries. She also used the device of *chryssónima* with the greater freedom which was characteristic of her period. The feathers of the angels' wings are worked in fine gold wire laid flat against a background of twisted gold thread, which produced a darker effect by contrast. She used Despoineta's method of shading the flesh parts and in some cases Despoineta's star-patterned halo.

An iconographically archaic detail is the fact that the Virgin leans over Christ from behind the bier instead of sitting at His head, which in general only occurs in the very early examples. It is typical of Theodosia's maladroit layout that the Cross with the lance and sponge should have to be cut off at the top, while one of the Magdalene's hands appears to grow out of Gabriel's shoulder, and the attempt at perspective is decidedly shaky. Nevertheless this piece has much that is beautiful in it. Even the Instruments of the Passion, surrounded by charming flower sprays, take on a decorative quality. The handsome floral border is more ornate than is usual in Greek work, and recalls the embroideries of the Three Hierarchs a hundred years earlier.

A very late epitaphios still in Despoineta's style is that of Kokona tou Rologa,[179] dated 1829, which came from the parish of Baphra near Samsun in Asia Minor. The gold is heavily padded and the working rather coarse, while the attitudes and expressions, although realistic, are over sentimental.

118

Meanwhile in the north of Serbia Christopher Žefarović was combining the classical elements of the epitaphios with his feeling for the baroque. The epitaphios illustrated, dated 1752, and commissioned, like the podea and curtain discussed earlier, by Constantine Brăncoveanu, is one of three which survive, all very much in the same style.

119, 120

Ignoring tradition, Žefarović has put Nicodemus at the head of the bier to balance Joseph of Arimathea at the foot. The Virgin bends forward to kiss the face of Christ, and St. John's position holding His hand has been taken by one of the mourning women, while St. John himself has been relegated to the background. The angels have joined the mourners instead of standing guard. The whole large group is held together by the Magdalene's expressive gesture which is wholly baroque, and a far cry from the realism of the Magdalene of Neamţ. Scenes of Jerusalem and Golgotha have been added in the background, and every possible iconographical detail, including the lamps which properly belong to the ciborium.

[179] Benaki Museum, Ἐκκλησιαστικὰ Κεντήματα, No. 92.
[180] Catalogue, Hristofor Žefarović, 1961, p. 66.

The baroque border and the circlets which surround the Evangelists occur in all Žefarović's epitaphioi, and are part of the trend which was current in all the embroideries of the eighteenth century towards a decorative rather than a purely pictorial style.

APPENDIX ONE

SHORT LIST OF EMBROIDERED VESTMENTS

HIERARCHICAL
VESTMENTS

Sticharion. The liturgical under-vestment, worn by all clergy. The western alb.

Epimanikia. Cuffs, worn by bishops and derived from ornament on the wrists of the sticharion. There is no western equivalent.

Phelonion. The liturgical over-vestment, worn by all priests. The western chasuble. In the middle ages the phelonion of a bishop was decorated all over with crosses and called *polystavrion*.

Saccos. A tunic-like garment with wide sleeves, worn in the middle ages by selected patriarchs only, later by all bishops. No western equivalent.

Mitra. The western mitre. Until the end of the middle ages it was worn in the eastern church only by the Patriarch of Alexandria.

Deacons in the Orthodox church wear the sticharion. There is no eastern vestment comparable to the dalmatic.

PRIESTLY
INSIGNIA

Epitrachilion. The priest's stole, worn by all priests and bishops. The two sides are joined all down the front. In later examples the neck is shaped like a collar.

Orarion. The deacon's stole. One long narrow strip worn over the left shoulder.

Omophorion. The insignia of a bishop. A long scarf-like strip decorated with applied crosses or circles, worn across the shoulders. The western pallium.

Epigonation. A stiffened square suspended from the girdle by one corner, worn by bishops. It derived from the ceremonial cloth or handkerchief which in the west developed into the maniple.

LITURGICAL VESTMENTS	**Endytí.** Altar cloth. Comparable to the western frontal, but covers the whole table.
	Eilitón. Early altar covering now replaced by the
	Antiminsion. Originally a consecrated cloth used to cover a temporary or makeshift altar. Later used on a fixed altar as well. Probably never embroidered, but painted or printed.
	Aër. Veil for the Communion vessels. The Little Aëres were used to cover chalice and patten separately, the Great Aër to cover both together. The Great Aër developed into the
	Epitaphios Sindon. A large veil decorated with the Body of the Crucified Christ which is carried in procession in the Good Friday services. Usually called simply *epitaphios*.
CHURCH FURNISHINGS	**Iconostasis curtain (katapetasma).** Curtains were originally hung between the pillars of the ciborium, and later used to cover the Royal Door (the central door) in the iconostasis. They are opened to reveal the holy mysteries at certain points in the service.
	Podea. A cloth hung below an icon as a gesture of reverence and honour. It was usually decorated with a scene complementary to that of the icon.
	Tomb covers. They appear to have been popular in Russia, and in Rumania in the fifteenth and sixteenth centuries. They were sometimes decorated with an embroidered effigy of the deceased person.

TRANS-LITERATION	GREEK / OLD SLAVONIC	MODERN GREEK	FIGURES	TRANS-LITERATION	GREEK / OLD SLAVONIC	MODERN GREEK	FIGURES
a	λ	Aα	1	s	Ϲ	Σ σ s	200
b	Б			t	Т	T τ	300
v	В	B β	2	i, y	Υ	Y υ	400
g	Г	Γ γ	3	ou	Ȣ OY		
d	Д	Δ δ	4	f (ph)	Ф	Φ φ	500
e	Є	E ε	5	kh	Х	X χ	600
zh	Ж			ps	Ѱ	Ψ ψ	700
z {	S Ϛ	(stigma) Τ, Ϛ	6	o	Ѡ	Ω ω	800
	З	Z ξ	7	ts	Ц	(sampi) ϡ	900
i {	Η Gr.	H η	8	ch	Ч	(koppa) ϟ, ϟ	90
	И Sl.			sh	Ш		
th	Ѳ	θ θ	9	sht	Щ		
i	I	I ι	10	'mute'	Ъ		
k	К	K κ	20	y	Ы		
l	Λ	Λ λ	30	'soft' sign	Ь		
m	М	M μ	40	ê	Ѣ		
n {	N Gr.	N ν	50	yu	Ю		
	Н Sl.			ya	Ѩ		
x	Ѯ	Ξ ξ	60	ya (nasal)	Ѧ	also 900 Sl.	
o	O	O ο	70				
p	П	Π π	80				
r	Р	P ρ	100				

BIBLIOGRAPHY

The first two sections of this bibliography are necessarily extremely selective. I have tried to make the section on embroidery as complete as possible. Certain other articles on specific embroideries, in Greek and the East Eurpean languages, published in ecclesiastical and archaeological periodicals which are not readily available in libraries in western Europe, are included in the bibliography of T. Papas, Studien zur Geschichte der Messgewänder (see below).

SUGGESTIONS FOR READING ON THE BYZANTINE BACKGROUND

BECKWITH, John, *The Art of Constantinople*, London 1961.

BYRON, R. and TALBOT RICE, D., *The Birth of Western Painting*, London 1930.

DALTON, O. M., *East Christian Art*, Oxford 1925.

DIEHL, C., *Manuel d'art byzantin*, Paris 1925.

EBERSOLT, J., *Les arts somptuaires de Byzance*, Paris 1923.

MATHEW, Gervase, *Byzantine Aesthetics*, London 1963.

MICHELIS, P. A., *An Aesthetic Approach to Byzantine Art*, English edition, London 1955.

RUNCIMAN, S., *Byzantine Civilisation*, London 1933.

TALBOT RICE, D., *Byzantine Art*, Oxford 1935.

—— *The Byzantines*, London 1962.

ZERNOV, N., *Eastern Christendom*, London 1961.

VESTMENTS

BRAUN, Joseph S. J., *Die liturgische Gewandung im Occident v. Orient*, Freiburg 1907.

—— *Der christliche Altar in seiner geschichtlichen Entwicklung*, Munich 1924.

—— *Die liturgische Gewandung in den Riten des Ostens* in STIMMEN AUS MARIA LAACH, 59, 1900, pp. 167-193.

KING, A. A., *The Rites of Eastern Christendom*, Rome 1947.

KURKULA, K., Τὰ ἱερατικὰ ἄμφια καὶ ὁ σνμβολισμὸς αὐτῶν ἐν τῇ Ὀρθοδόξῳ Ἑλληνικῇ ἐκκλησίᾳ, Athens 1960,

PAPAS, T., *Studien zur Geschichte der Messgewänder im Byzantinischen Ritus*, Munich 1965.

SALAVILLE, S., *An Introduction to the Study of Eastern Liturgies*, trs. from the French by J. M. T. Barton, London 1938.

TRENKLE, Elisabeth, *Liturgische Geräte und Gewänder der Ostkirche*, Slavisches Institut, Munich 1962.

EMBROIDERY

ACADEMIA REPUBLICII POPULARE ROMINE, *Repertoriul Monumentelor şi Obiectelor de Artă din Timpul lui Ştefan cel Mare*, Bucharest 1958. (Quoted as *A.R.P.R.*, *Répertoriul.*)

—— *Studii asupra Tezaurului restituit de A.R.S.S.*, Bucharest 1958. (Quoted as *A.R.P.R.*, *Studii.*)

—— *Cultura Moldovenească in Timpul lui Ştefan cel Mare*, Bucharest 1964. (Quoted as *A.R.P.R. Cultura Moldovenească.*)

BENAKI MUSEUM (Eugenia Hadjidakis), Ἐκκλησιαστικὰ Κεντήματα, Athens 1953.

BEZA, Marcu, *Byzantine Art in Rumania*, London 1940.

BOSTON MUSEUM OF FINE ARTS, *Some Greek Liturgical Embroideries*, BULLETIN XLII, 1944.

BRAUN, Joseph, S. J., *La Dalmatique du Trésor de St. Pierre*, in REVUE DE L'ART CHRETIEN, 1901, p. 52.

CANALE, Mich. Giuseppe, *Discorso intorno al Pallio de seta, lavoro bizantino del sec. XIII*, in DESCRIZIONE DI GENOVA E DEL GENOVESATO, Vol. III, 1846.

CATALOGUE, *Exposition de l'art roumain ancien et moderne*, Musée du Jeu de Paume, Paris 1925.

—— *Catalogul expozitiei de argintărie, broderii si ţesături din Tara Romînească, Sec. XVI-XVII*, Bucharest 1956.

—— *Hristofor Žefarović*, Galerija Matice Srpske, Novi Sad, 1961.

—— *Byzantine Art, 9th Exhibition of the Council of Europe*, Athens 1964.

—— *Rumanian Art Treasures, XV-XVIIIth centuries*, Edinburgh/London, 1965/6.

DOLGER, Franz, *Zwei byzantinischen Fahnen im Halberstädter Domschatz*, in BEITRÄGE ZUR GESCHICHTE DER PHILISOPHIE DES MITTELALTERS, Supplement Band 3, pt. II, 1935.

DRAGHICEANU, Virgil, *Un epitaf al mitropolitului Ştefan*, in BULETINUL COMISIUNII MONUMENTELOR ISTORICE XXII, Bucharest 1929.

FARCY, Louis de, *La broderie de l'XIième siècle jusqu'à nos jours*, Paris 1890.

FROLOV, A., *La podéa*, in BYZANTION, Vol. 13, 1938.

GOSHEV, N., *Antiminsŭt*, Sofia 1935.

GRIGORAŞ, N., *Biserica Trei Ierarhi din Iaşi*, Jassy 1962.

HADJIMICHAELI, Angeliki, Τὰ χρυσοκλαβαρικὰ-συρματέϊνα-συρμακεσικα κεντήματα in MÉLANGES MERLIER, Vol. II, pp. 447-499, Institut Français d'Athènes, 1956.

IORGA, N., *Les Arts mineurs en Roumanie*, Bucharest 1936.

—— *Tapiţeriile doamnei Tudosca a lui Vasile Lupu*, in BULETINUL COMISIUNII MONUMENTELOR ISTORICE VIII, p. 147, Bucharest 1915.

—— *Patrahirul lui Alexandru cel Bun*, in ANALELE ACADEMIEI ROMINE XXXV, Bucharest 1912-13.

JACOPI, Giulio, *Cimeli del Ricamo, della Pittura e della Toreutica nel Tesoro del Monastero di Patmo*, in CLARA RHODOS, Studi e Materiali, Inst. Storico Archeol. di Rodi, Vol. VII, 1933.

JANKOVIĆ, Dušan, *The Nun Euphemia*, trs. H. M. Stansfield Popović, The Yugoslav Association of University Women, Belgrade 1936.

JERPHANION, Guillaume de, *Le trésor de Putna et les peintures de Cappadoce*, in L'ART BYZANTIN CHEZ LES SLAVES, III, pp. 310-314, Paris 1930.

JOHNSTONE, P., *Church Embroidery in Rumania*, in REVUE ROUMAINE D'HISTOIRE DE L'ART, I, Bucharest 1964.

—— *The Embroideries of Christopher Žefarović*, in APOLLO, March 1964.

—— *Church Embroideries in the Exhibition of Rumanian Art Treasures*, in EMBROIDERY, Vol. 17, No. 2, 1966.

KONDAKOV, N. P., *Makedoniya*, St. Petersburg 1909.

LEMBERG, Mechthild, *Zum Antependium von Grandson*, Bern, HISTORISCHES MUSEUM JAHRBUCH 1957-8, p. 143.

LE TOURNEAU, M. and MILLET, G., *Un chef-d'oeuvre de la broderie byzantine* (the Salonica epitaphios), in BULLETIN DE CORRESPONDANCE HELLÉNIQUE, Ecole français d'Athènes, XXIX, 1905, pp. 259-268.

MIGEON, Gaston, *Les arts du tissu*, Paris 1929.

MILLET, Gabriel, *Broderies religieuses de style byzantin*, Paris 1947. (Quoted as *Millet, Broderies.*)

—— *La Dalmatique du Vatican*, Paris, 1945. (Quoted as *Millet, La Dalmatique.*)

——*Dédicace grecque d'une broderie moldave*, in MÉLANGES FR. MARTROYE, Société Nationale des Antiquaires, Paris 1941.

MILLET, G.; PARGOIRE, J.; PETIT, L., *Recueil des inscriptions chrétiennes de l'Athos*, Paris 1904.

MIRKOVIC, L., *Crkveni Umetnički Vez*, Belgrade 1940.

—— *Monahinja Jefimija*, Sremski Karlovci 1922.

MIYATEV, K., *Sukrovishtnitsata na Rilskiya Monastir*, in GODISHNIK NA NARODNIYA MUSEÎ, Sofia 1922-25 (1 vol.), p. 314.

MOSCOW KREMLIN, MUSEUM OF THE PALACE OF ARMS, *Uskusstvo Vizantii, V-XV vekov.*

MUÑOZ, A., *L'art byzantin à l'exposition de Grottaferrata*, Rome 1906.

MUZICESCU, Maria Ana, *Portretul laic brodat in arta medievală romînească*, in STUDII ȘI CERCETĂRI DE ISTORIA ARTEI IX, Bucharest 1962.

—— *La broderie roumaine au moyen-âge*, in REVUE ROUMAINE D'HISTOIRE DE L'ART I, 1964.

NICOLESCU, Corina, *Moldavian Embroideries of the 15th-18th centuries in the collection of the R.P.R. Art Museum*, Bucharest 1964.

PROTIĆ, A., *Denatsionalizirane i Vŭzrazhdane na nasheto Izkustvo ot 1393 do 1879 god.*, in BULGARIYA 1000 GODINI, Sofia 1927, pp. 383-540.

ROHAULT DE FLEURY, *La Messe, Etudes archéologiques sur ses monuments*, Paris 1881-9.

ROTHEMUND, B., *Byzantinische und russische kirchliche Stickereien*, Slavisches Institut München. Munich 1961.

SACHSEN, Johann Georg, Herzog zu, *Kunstschätze im Sinaikloster*, in ZEITSCHRIFT FÜR CHRISTLICHE KUNST 1911, pp. 299-304.

SOTIRIOU, G., *Guide du Musée Byzantin d'Athènes*, trs. O. Merlier, Athens 1932.

——Κειμήλια τοῦ Οἰκουμενικοῦ Πατριαρχείου, Athens 1938.

——Τὰ λειτουργικὰ ἄμφια τῆς Ὀρθοδόξου Ἑλληνικῆς Ἐκκλησίας, in θεολογία, Κ, pp. 603-614, Athens 1949.

SOTIRIOU, Maria, Χρνσοκεντητον ἐπιγονάτιον τοῦ Βυζαντινοῦ Μουσειοῦ, in
Πρακτικὰ Χριστιανικῆς Ἀρχαιολογικῆς Ἑταιρίας, Β, Athens 1936.
STEFANEȘCU, I. D., *La peinture religieuse en Bucovine et en Moldavie*, Paris 1928. (Quoted
as *Ștefanescu*, La Peinture.)
—— *La voile de calice brodée de Vatra-Moldovitei*, in ART BYZANTIN CHEZ LES SLAVES,
LES BALKANS I, 1930, p. 303.
—— *L'illustration des liturgies dans l'art de Byzance et de l'Orient*, Institut de Philologie
et d'Histoire Orientales, Brussels 1936.
—— *Voiles d'iconostase, tentures de ciboire, äers, äers ou voiles de procession*, in ANALECTA,
UNIVERSITATEA DIN BUCUREȘTI, Institutul de Istoria Artei, I, 1943. (Quoted as
Ștefanescu, Voiles.)
—— *Autels, tissus et broderies liturgiques*, in ANALECTA, UNIVERSITATEA DIN BUCUREȘTI,
Institutul de Istoria Artei, II, 1944.
—— *L'äer de la princesse Malina*, in REVISTÂ ISTORÎCĂ ROMÎNĂ, XV, Bucharest 1945.
STOJANOVIĆ, Dobrila, *Umetnički Vez u Srbiji od XIV do XIX veka*, Belgrade 1959.
(Quoted as, *Stojanović, Umetnički Vez*.)

TAFRALI, O., *Le trésor byzantin et roumain du monastère de Poutna*, Paris 1925. (Quoted
as *Tafrali, Putna*.)
—— *Le monastère de Sucevița et son trésor*, in MÉLANGES CHARLES DIEHL, Etudes sur
l'histoire et sur l'art de Byzance II, p. 207, Paris 1930. (Quoted as *Tafrali, Sucevita*.)
THEOCARIS, M. Ἐκκλησιαστικὰ ἄμφια τῆς μονῆς Τατάρνης in θεολογία 27, 1956, pp.
123-147.
—Ἀνέκοτα ἄμφια τῆς μονῆς Φανερωμένης Σαλαμῖνος in θεολογία 27, 1956,
pp. 325-333.
——Ἀφιερωτικαὶ ἐπιγραφαὶ ἐπὶ ἀμφίων τοῦ ῞Αθω in θεολογὶα 28, 1957, pp.
452-456.
——Ὑπογραφαὶ κεντητῶν ἐπὶ ἀμφίων τοῦ ῞Αθω in Ἐπετηρὶς Ἑταιρίας
Βυζαντινῶν Σπουῶν 32, 1963, pp. 496-503.
TURDEANU, Emil, *La broderie religieuse en Roumanie: les épitaphes moldaves aux 15me et
16me siècles*, in CERCETĂRI LITERARE, Vol. 4, pp. 164-214, Bucharest 1940.
—— *La broderie religieuse en Roumanie: les étoles des XVme et XVIme siecles*, in BULETINUL
INSTITUTULUI ROMIN DIN SOFIA I, pp. 5-61, Bucharest 1941. (Quoted as *Turdeanu,
Les étoles*.)

VASILIĆ, Angelika, *Riznica manastira Studenice*, Belgrade 1957.

VĂTĂȘIĂNU, V., *L'arte bizantina in Romania. I ricami liturgici*. Rome 1945.
VICTORIA & ALBERT MUSEUM, *Early Christian and Byzantine Art*, London 1949.

WACE, A. *An epitaphios in London*, in Εἰς μνήμην Σπυρίδωνος Λάμπρου p. 232-235.
Athens 1935.

INDEX

(The bold figures refer to the illustrations)

1. The Vatican Saccos, *The Calling of the Chosen*, 14th century. (Treasury of St. Peter's, Rome.)

2. The Vatican Saccos, *The Transfiguration*, 14th century. (Treasury of St. Peter's, Rome.)

3.   The Vatican Saccos, *Communion of the Apostles.*   (see Pl. 1.)   (Treasury of St. Peter's, Rome.)

4. The Vatican Saccos.   Detail of Pl. 1.

5. The Vatican Saccos. Detail of Pl. 1, *The Chosen*.

6. The Vatican Saccos. Detail of Pl. 2, *St. Peter*.

7. The Great Saccos of Photius. Early 15th century.
(Museum of the Moscow Kremlin, Palace of Arms.)

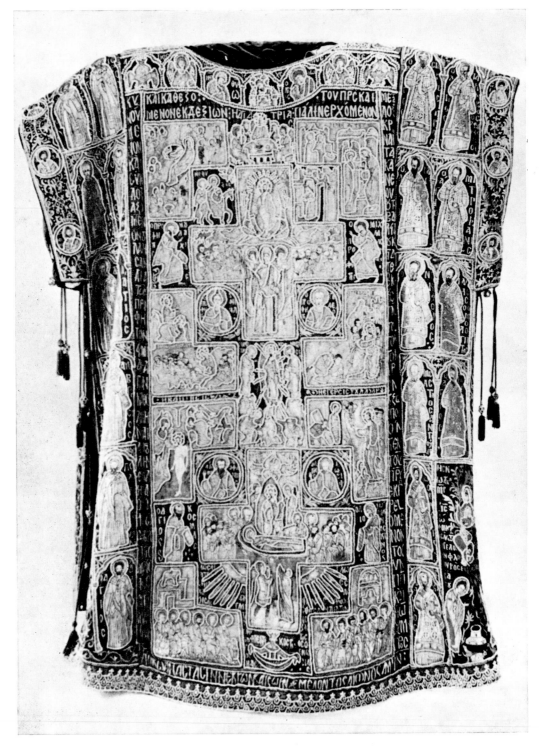

8. The Great Saccos of Photius. Early 15th century.
(Museum of the Moscow Kremlin, Palace of Arms.)

9.   Detail of Pl. 7.   *The Grand Prince Vassili Dmitrievitch and*
Princess Sophia Vitovtovna.

10.   Detail of Pl. 7.   *The Metropolitan Photius.*

11.   The Little Saccos of Photius.   14th/early 15th century.
(Museum of the Moscow Kremlin, Palace of Arms.)

12. The Little Saccos of Photius. 14th/early 15th century.
(Museum of the Moscow Kremlin, Palace of Arms.)

13. Detail of Pl. 11. *The Crucifixion.*

14. Detail of Pl. 11. *The Anastasis.*

15. Saccos designed by Christopher Žefarović. 1751.
(Museum of Art, Bucharest.)

16. Mitre. Late 16th/17th century.
(Monastery of St. John the Divine, Patmos.)

17. Mitre. 1715. (Benaki Museum, Athens.)

ΔΕΗCΙC ΤΧ ΔΧΛΧ ΤΧ ΘΕΧ ΔΙΟΝΥCΙΑ ΤΑΡΡΩΝΎΤΧ ·
ΧΕΙΡ ΠΑΡΘΕΝΙΧ ΙΕΡΟΜΟΝΑΧΧ ΚΑΓΓΕΛΑΡΙ ΕΞΑ ΘΗΝΩΝ · 17Λ9· Μαστιγα

18. Icon. *St.Dionysius the Areopagite.* 1729.
(The Hellenic Institute, Venice.)

19-21. Epimanikia. 16th century.
(Byzantine Museum, Athens.)

22-23. Epimanikia, *The Annunciation.* 1608.
(Byzantine Museum, Athens.)

24. Epimanikion from Vintilă-Vodă. 16th century. (Museum of Art, Bucharest.)

25. Epimanikion from Govora. Early 16th century. (Museum of Art, Bucharest.)

26. Epimanikion. Detail, *The Angel of the Annunciation.*
16th century. (see also Pl. 27.) (Museum of Art, Bucharest.)

27. Epimanikion. Detail, *The Virgin of the Annunciation.*
16th century. (see also Pl. 26.) (Museum of Art, Bucharest.)

28. Epimanikion. *The Salutation.* 18th century.
(Museum of Greek Popular Art, Athens.)

29. Epitrachilion from Bistriţa. *The Great Feasts.*
First half 15th century. (Museum of Art, Bucharest.)

30. Detail of Pl. 29. *The Baptism*.

31. Epitrachilion. Detail, *The Virgin*. First half 15th century. (see also Pls. 32-4.)
(Monastery of St. John the Divine, Patmos.)

32. Epitrachilion. Detail, *St. John the Baptist*. First half 15th century.
(see also Pls. 31, 33-4.) (Monastery of St. John the Divine, Patmos.)

33. Epitrachilion. Detail of ornament. First half 15th century. (see also Pls. 31-2, 34.)
(Monastery of St. John the Divine, Patmos.)

34. Epitrachilion. Detail of ornament. First half 15th century. (see also Pls. 31-3.)
(Monastery of St. John the Divine, Patmos.)

35. Epitrachilion. *The Great Feasts*. Gift of Stephen the Great and Alexander to Putna,
1478-80. (see also Pl. 36.) (Monastery of Putna.)

36.   Epitrachilion.   *The Great Feasts*.   Gift of Stephen the Great and Alexander to Putna, 1478-80.   (see also Pl. 35.)   (Monastery of Putna.)

37. Epitrachilion. Gift of Stephen the Great and Maria to Putna. Early 16th century.
(Monastery of Putna.)

38. Epitrachilion. Late 15th century. (Treasury of Aachen Cathedral.)

39. Detail of Pl. 37. *Solomon*.

40. Epitrachilion from Dobrovaţ. Detail, *Stephen the Great*. Early 16th century.
(see also Pl. 41.) (Museum of Art, Bucharest.)

41. Epitrachilion from Dobrovaţ. Detail, *The Princess Maria Voichiţa*.
Early 16th century. (see also Pl. 40.) (Museum of Art, Bucharest.)

42. Epitrachilion. Gift of Barbu Craiovescu and Neagoslava to Bistriţa, 1521. Detail, *The Donors*. (Museum of Art, Bucharest.)

43. Epitrachilion. Mid-16th century. (Victoria and Albert Museum, London.)

44. Epitrachilion. 16th century. (Byzantine Museum, Athens.)

45. Epitrachilion from Cotroceni. Detail. 17th century.
(Museum of Art, Bucharest.)

46. Epitrachilion from Hurezi worked by Despoineta. Detail. 1696.
(Museum of Art, Bucharest—Mogoşoaia.)

47. Epitrachilion designed by
Christopher Žefarović. 1750.
(Museum of Art, Bucharest.)

48. Orarion. The gift of Radu Paisie, 1538.
(Victoria and Albert Museum, London.)

49. Cross from an omophorion. *The Anastasis*. Late 15th/early 16th century.
(Monastery of St. John the Divine, Patmos.)

50. Omophorion. 1618. (Abbey of Grottaferrata.)

51. Epigonation. *The Anastasis*. 13th/early 14th century.
(Byzantine Museum, Athens.)

52. Epigonation (?). *The Christ Child*. 14th century.
(Monastery of St. John the Divine, Patmos.)

53. Epigonation. *The Transfiguration*. Late 16th/17th century.
(Byzantine Museum, Athens.)

54. Epigonation. *The Washing of Feet*. 1587. (Victoria and Albert Museum, London.)

55. Epigonation. *The Adoration of the Magi*, worked by Despoineta, 1696. (Benaki Museum, Athens.)

56. Sanctuary hanging or podea. *The Ascension*. 1484. (Monastery of Putna.)

57. Sanctuary hanging or podea. *The Dormition of the Virgin*. 1485. (Monastery of Putna.)

58. Detail of Pl. 57.

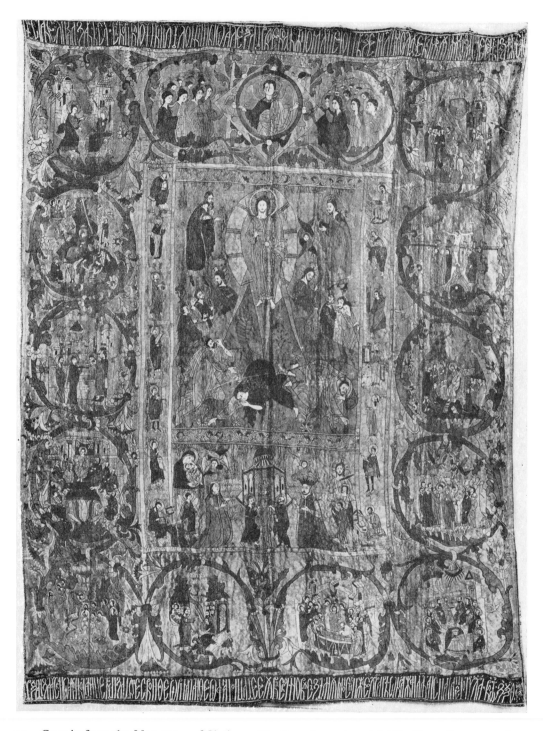

59. Curtain from the Monastery of Slatina. *The Transfiguration* with *The Great Feasts*. 1561.
(Museum of Art, Bucharest.)

60.   Detail of Pl. 59.   *The Donors.*

61. Detail of Pl. 59. *The Annunciation.*

62.   Detail of Pl. 59.   *The Entry into Jerusalem.*

63. Curtain from the Monastery of Slatina. *The Transfiguration.* 1561.
(Museum of Art, Bucharest.)

64.   Detail of Pl. 63.   *The Donor, Alexander Lăpușneanu.*

65. Detail of Pl. 63. *The Princess Roxanda.*

66. Curtain. *The Annunciation* with *The Great Feasts*, signed by the Nun Agni.
Mid-16th century. (Museum of Decorative Art, Belgrade.)

67.   Curtain from the Monastery of Staneşti.   *The Crucifixion.*
Late 16th century.   (Museum of Art, Bucharest.)

68. Curtain from the Church of the Three Hierarchs,
Jassy. *St. Peter*. 1638.
(Museum of Art, Bucharest.)

69. Podea from the Church of the Three Hierarchs, Jassy.
The Annunciation. 1638. (Museum of Art, Bucharest.)

70.   Curtain from the Church of the Three Hierarchs, Jassy.   1639.
(Museum of Art, Bucharest.)

71. Curtain. *The Vision of Ezekiel*, designed by Christopher Žefarović, 1752. (Museum of Art, Bucharest.)

72. Detail of Pl. 71.

73. Podea. *The Coronation of the Virgin*, designed by Christopher Žefarović, 1752.
(Museum of Art, Bucharest.)

74. Detail of curtain. *The Archangel Michael*, designed by Christopher Žefarović, 18th century. (Museum of Art, Bucharest.)

75. Embroidered icon. *St. George and the Dragon*, signed by the Nun Agatha, 1729.
(Benaki Museum, Athens.)

76.   Embroidered icon.   *St. George and the Dragon,* signed by Theodosia Kasymbouri, 1731.
(Benaki Museum, Athens.)

77. Podea. *The Creed.* 1736. (Museum of Greek Popular Art, Athens.)

78. Pall. The Princess Euphemia's *Laud to Prince Lazar.* 1402.
(Museum of the Serbian Orthodox Church, Belgrade.)

79.   Tomb cover of Maria of Mangop.   After 1477.
(Monastery of Putna.)

80. Detail of Pl. 79.

81. Tomb cover of Jeremiah Movila. After 1606.
(Monastery of Suceviţa.)

82.   Tomb cover of Simeon Movila.   1609.
(Monastery of Sucevița.)

83. Tomb cover of Tudosca, wife of Basil Lupu. Mid-17th century.
(Church of the Three Hierarchs, Jassy.)

84. Tomb cover of John, son of Basil Lupu. Mid-17th century.
(Church of the Three Hierarchs, Jassy.)

85. Aër. *The Communion of the Apostles.* Late 12th century.
(Halberstadt Cathedral.) (see also Pl. 86.)

86. Aër. *The Communion of the Apostles.* Late 12th century.
(Halberstadt Cathedral.) (see also Pl. 85.)

87.   Aër. *The Communion of the Apostles*. Early 14th century.
(see also Pl. 88.) (The Collegiate Church of Castell' Arquato.)

88. Aër. *The Communion of the Apostles.* Early 14th century. (see also Pl. 87.)
(The Collegiate Church of Castell' Arquato.)

89. Aër. *The Communion*. 14th century. (Benaki Museum, Athens.)

90. Aër. *The Communion of the Apostles.* Gift of Stephen the Great to Radauți, 1493.
(Monastery of Suceviṭa.)

91.   Aër.   *The Christ Child*.   17th century.   (Benaki Museum, Athens.)

92. Fresco. The epitaphios in the procession of the Great Entry. 16th century.
(Monastery church of Kaisariani, Athens.)

93.   The St. Clement epitaphios *c.*1295.   (Present whereabouts unknown.)

94.   The epitaphios of Milutin Ureš.   *c*.1300.
(Museum of the Serbian Orthodox Church, Belgrade.)

95. The Salonica epitaphios. 14th century. (see also Pl. 96 and Frontispiece.) (Byzantine Museum, Athens.)

96. Detail of Pl. 95.

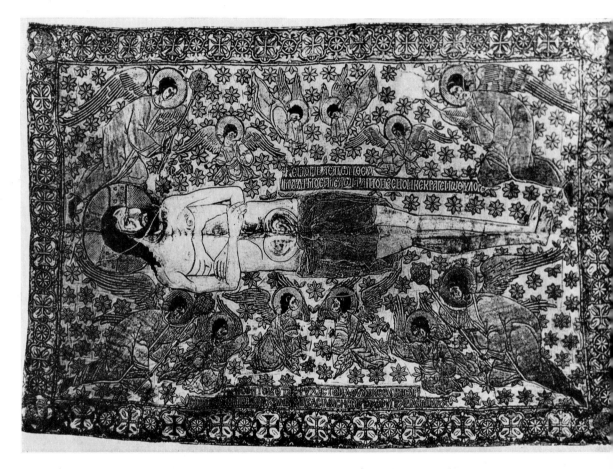

97. The epitaphios of Eupemia and Eupraxia. Late 14th century. (Monastery of Putna.)

98. Epitaphios. 14th century. (Basilica of St. Mark, Venice.)

99. The epitaphios of Nicholas Eudaimonoioannes. 1407. (Victoria and Albert Museum, London.)

100.   Detail of Pl. 99.

101. The Cozia epitaphios. 1396. (Museum of Art, Bucharest.)

102. The Neamţ epitaphios. 1437. (Museum of Art, Bucharest.)

103. Detail of Pl. 102. *The mourning angel.*

104. Detail of Pl. 102. *St. Mary Magdalene*.

105.   The aër of Pope Anastasius.   1484.   (Monastery of Vatra-Moldoviţei.)

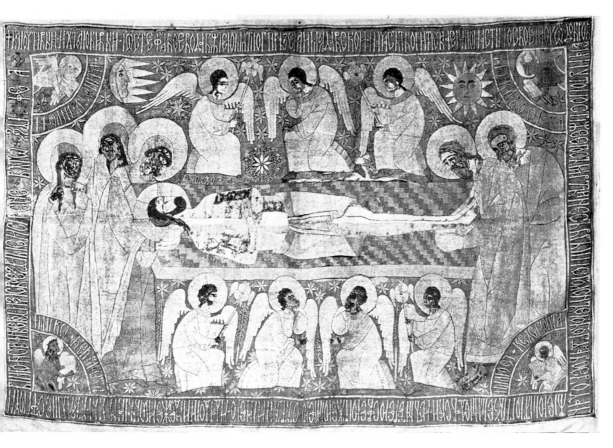

106. The Dobrovaţ epitaphios. 1506. (Museum of Art, Bucharest.)

107. Detail of Pl. 106.

108. The Slatina epitaphios. 1556. (Museum of Art, Bucharest.)

109. Detail of Pl. 108.

110. Epitaphios worked by the Nun Philothea. 1608. (Monastery of Secu.)

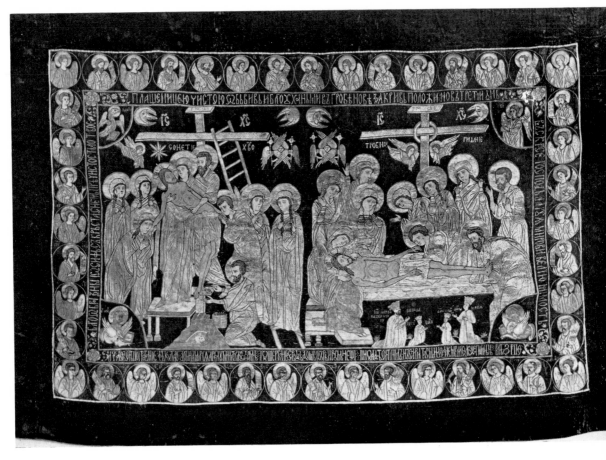

111.   Epitaphios of Prince Șerban Cantacuzene.   1681.   (Museum of Art, Bucharest.)

112. Epitaphios of Syrianothomas. 17th century. (Benaki Museum, Athens.)

113. Epitaphios worked by Despoineta. 1682. (Benaki Museum, Athens.)

114.   Detail of Pl. 113.

115. Epitaphios worked by Despoineta and Alexandra. 1712. (Victoria and Albert Museum, London.)

116.   Epitaphios worked by Theodosia Kasymbouri.   1738.   (Benaki Museum, Athens.)

117. Detail of Pl. 116.

118. Epitaphios worked by Kokona tou Rologa. 1829. (Benaki Museum, Athens.)

119. Epitaphios designed by Christopher Žefarović. 1752. (Museum of Art, Bucharest.)

120.   Detail of Pl. 119.